# The Rhythm of Learning
## Discovering the Power of Music in Montessori Education

Margarita Shvets & Raymond Aaron

Copyright © 2016 by Margarita Shvets & Raymond Aaron

No part of this publication may be reproduced or transmitted in any form, or by electronic or mechanical means, including any information storage or retrieval system, without permission in writing from the publisher.

ISBN-13: 978-1-77277-047-6 (Print Edition)
ISBN-13: 978-1-77277-048-3 (e-book)

Published by
10-10-10 Publishing
Markham, Ontario
CANADA

# Contents

| | |
|---|---|
| Testimonials | v |
| Acknowledgements | ix |
| Foreword | xi |
| Chapter One (do) | 1 |
| Chapter Two (re) | 19 |
| Chapter Three (mi) | 43 |
| Chapter Four (fa) | 53 |
| Chapter Five (sol) | 63 |
| Chapter Six (la) | 77 |
| Chapter Seven (ti) | 89 |
| Conclusion | 101 |

# Testimonials

Professional Referral: Ms. Margarita Shvets

My Dear Margarita

It is with a happy and proud heart that I am able to harness these words I write about you, and the sheer delight and pleasure with which I use them to tell the world what I think about you is priceless.

By no means was this a task to figure out what words could be best suited or which one could I place in front of another. No! Instead I let my heart dictate the words as I transposed them onto the page.

As a staunch proponent of supporting education within Miami-Dade County, Miami, Florida through the local aviation and aerospace business community, and being a recognized and known public and business leader figure within South Florida who champions for the fostering, encouragement and growth of aerospace education via the County school system Science, Technology, Engineering and Math (STEM) program, I Mr. Benny F. Benitez, Founder and CEO of the 94th AeroClaims-Aviation Consultant Group wish to render a proper recommendation toward my friend and colleague Ms. Margarita Shvets.

The approach that Ms. Shvets creates and applies to her students within the realm of musical training via her Montessori approach is exemplary worthy of being established as a National standard.

Her recent publication *The Rhythm of Learning* is a worthwhile read and must for the collection of any educator who seeks to focus on the application of musical instructions toward young children.

Words like "astonishing" and "remarkable" are often evoked toward the attributes that one could apply when describing the magic that is created by Ms. Shvets when she applies her tutelage to very young children and is therefore able to tap a level of learning that is paramount and forever life changing.

The Rhythm of Music could very well be as important to society in developmental learning as the teaching of Sigmund Freud.
**-Mr. Benny Benitez Founder & CEO of the 94th AeroClaims-Aviation Consultant Group.**
**FAA A&P Lic., DoD Consultant**
**Chair of the George T. Baker Aviation Technical College Industry Steering Committee**
**Aviation Adviser to U.S. Southern Command (J-9), FBI-Miami / INFRAGARD, Miami-Dade Police Department Special Response Team**
**Bank Approved Aviation Equipment Appraiser**

Mrs. Rita Shvets combines the two great cultures of the piano skills, i.e. Russian and American—Leonard Bernstein and Valentin Silvestrov. Mrs. Shvets talent or gift of teaching has no comparison.
**-Ewgeney Koifman**
**Professor, History of musical culture, Ethnography, Moscow**

5 stars! The most cheerful and peaceful Pre-school I ever visited. I definitely recommend parents to send their kids here. My son is so happy and looking forward to going to school every morning!
-Yvonne And Steve Chang
**Parents/Customers of Vernon Hills Montessori Academy**

This was the 5th school my daughter had been to. She was in the transition room and then the 3-6. I also had a son who was in the transition room simultaneously.

The owner's heart is where it should be and the teachers are amazing. They continuously stimulate their mind, body, and interests

They truly go above and beyond!
-**Bridget Nelson**
**Parents/Customers of Vernon Hills Montessori Academy**

"As a Montessori teacher, Margarita learned the importance of the crucial early years from birth to age six where children soak up everything like sponges, including music, if it is offered in the environment. She learned about timing and the importance of "sensitive periods", or developmental stages, to develop skills precisely at the right time. From matching and grading the Montessori bells, to writing music with the wooden Montessori notes and note boards, to singing and projecting the voice, and dancing with rhythm and rhyme, and playing Orff music instruments and the piano, the Montessori children had a rich and joyful music experience with Miss Margarita that they carried with them throughout life!"
-**Carolyn Kambich, Founder of Deerfield Montessori Schools Founder and Former President of American Illinois Montessori Society (AIMS), Living Legacy**

*Margarita Shvets & Raymond Aaron*

"Music with Margarita is Magical! Margarita inspires a love of music and learning, beginning with the very youngest children, at a time when children are most receptive to the discovery of language, music and melody. To see these children joyfully engaged is simply delightful! This book provides some wonderful insights for parents and teachers alike."
-**Lisa Kambich, Director of Schools, North Shore Montessori Schools**

# Acknowledgements

I want to say thank you to my former supervisor and mentor JOJI ESCANILA—during my first year of teaching in a Montessori school—for being so strict and firm with me while also letting me learn from her the techniques of Presentation and of making Montessori Materials and showing me that through hard and repetitive work the TRUE KNOWLEDGE and EXPERIENCE comes.

A special thank you to Carolyn, Lisa Kambich and Loise Kunnert for BELIEVING in me, for giving me the opportunity to start my Pedagogical Montessori Career in such a prestigious state-of-the-art Montessori school and also for providing the best Montessori Training in Illinois. Their continuous efforts in educating and mentoring me as I grew the foundation required to become an outstanding Montessori Directress and Music Teacher in a Montessori setting will always be remembered.

Thank you to my dear Montessori friends Charlene Alderete and Michael Rubino for being next to me through the MOST stressful time of my life—when going through a divorce from my husband and a separation with my business partners—and for being supportive mentally, emotionally, physically and financially.

Thank you to my piano teacher, Vassa Vasilievna Favorova, who inspired me to not quit and to become a great piano and music teacher.

Thank you to my Music and Pedagogic college teachers for helping to build my foundation for constant improvement.

*Margarita Shvets & Raymond Aaron*

Thank you to my wonderful teachers, teacher assistants, office manager and my most loyal piano students: Charlene McCloskey, Aloyna Foca, Ludmila Yankovsky, Raisa Greyz, Sandra Kolgoviene, Alex Stepul, Anna Kovalenko, Mervyn Raasch, Marika Ratkeviciute and Cindy Davis, Kathleen and Oz Ingrid, and Cynthia Batman for continuing to implement "The Rhythm of Learning Program" at the Vernon Hills Montessori Academy.

Thank you to all the school parents who allow me to work with, to inspire and to create in their children a tremendous love of music and a joy of learning.

And to my children: Paul Bourdel, Anthony and Masha Shvets and Ruslan Khamdulaev–thank you for always being loveable, PRESENT and appreciative, even though you see me with other children all the time.

Thank you to my dad, mom, sister and whole family for being proud of me at all times.

Thank you to my ex-husbands Nick Bourdel and Ivan Shvets for forgiving me....

Thank you to my girlfriends (for being patient with me): Tatyana Babenko, Tatiana Vodovoz, Nataliya Soboleva, Natasha Veselovsky, Natasha Klemetieva, Arina Stratievsky, Nursulu Shayahkmetova, Irina Kharlamova, Irina Pasternak, Galina Diomidova, Irina Hilkevich.

Thank you to my friends Tom Jikomes, Bear Harris and Anthony Atkinson for motivating/encouraging me to write this book.

# Foreword

My name is Louise Harrison. I'm the sister of George Harrison of The Beatles fame. Like George, I am passionate about music. A few years ago I started a program meant to save music programs in our schools called HELP KEEP MUSIC ALIVE. With so many schools losing their music programs, can you imagine my absolute surprise and joy to find a Montessori school—the first ever to do so—with a daily music program that includes children as young as 15 months of age! To listen to the music these young children make and to witness the love with which they approach that music was enough to bring tears to my eyes.

The pioneer behind this music curriculum (that sees children beginning their days with music) is Margarita Shvets, who has a Masters Degree in Music, specializing in piano teaching methods, choir conducting and music theory and a Masters Degree in Psychology and Methods of Primary Education. She is the Owner, Director and a Music Teacher at the Vernon Hills Montessori Academy in Vernon Hills, Illinois.

It has been scientifically proven that learning music boosts brain power, improves memory, builds social skills and confidence and teaches patience and expression. The approach that Ms. Shvets creates and applies to her students, within the realm of musical training via her Montessori approach, is exemplary and worthy of being established as a National standard. Her recent publication "The Rhythm of Learning" is a fantastic read and should be added to the collection of any educator who seeks to focus on the application of musical instructions toward young children.

Now Margarita has decided to write a book about her specialized music program in the Montessori style. It is called: *The Rhythm of Learning: Discovering the Power of Music in Montessori Education.* The target market is directors and teachers at other Montessori schools, parents of children in those schools or parents considering a Montessori school. Here are some of the topics it covers ...

**Montessori education** is an educational approach developed by Italian physician and educator Maria Montessori and is characterized by an emphasis on independence, freedom within limits, and respect for a child's natural psychological, physical, and social development. These schools share three essential elements: Mixed age classrooms, with classrooms for children ages 15 months to 3 years and/or 3 to 6 years (the most common); student choice of activity from within a prescribed range of options; and uninterrupted blocks of work time, ideally three hours. There is also an emphasis on freedom of movement within the classroom and the presence of a trained Montessori teacher.

**The Benefits of Music and Movement:** I was amazed to find that 88% of all post-graduate students in college and 83% of all people earning $150,000 or more had extensive music training.

Daycare versus Montessori Preschool: Here you learn about the length of classes, teaching and learning styles, tuition and much more.

**Margarita's Journey:** From Moscow to America and from teacher to owner, Margarita seems to have been destined to be a Montessori music pioneer.

**The Effectiveness of Music:** Here are just a few examples of the effectiveness of music training ... early musical training helps

*The Rhythm of Learning*

develop brain areas involved in language and reasoning. Students of the arts learn to think creatively and to solve problems. Music study enhances teamwork skills and discipline. It develops skills that are necessary in the workplace. Music performance also teaches young people to conquer fear and to take risks.

**The Montessori Approach to Music: What does the Montessori approach teach and provide?** It teaches that with the right experiences, all children can sing and carry a tune, all children can train their ears, all children can learn to read and write music. In other words, all children can participate in one of the basic expressions of what it means to be human, in the language of music.

**Why Every Day?** Quite simply, repetition is the basis of music learning, just as it is in any other language. A simple drop of water repeated over time can wear away stone. So, too, can daily music lessons instill in children the basic elements that form the foundation for success.

**The Earlier the Better!** Young children are like dry sponges. When you drop them in water they expand dramatically. So just as the child moves before he walks, so can the child sing before she talks. It's amazing to watch!

**The Steps to Joyful Learning:** The joyful experience that can be music starts with the parents. If they are positive in their talk and actions regarding the daily music classes, then it is much easier for the child to relax and develop a "home" at school.

**Spring, Sing. Winter Holiday Concert!** Many schools, Montessori or otherwise have just one, annual concert. However, Margarita believes in celebrating the seasons with song and music that can be shared with the parents. From

Halloween to Thanksgiving to Christmas and Spring, the children fall in love with the different songs of the seasons and can't wait to perform on stage (They don't know that they should be shy or frightened; it's just something that's fun to do.)

**Music at Home:** The greatest thing for a parent who is attuned to the child is the impromptu concert that he or she will experience at home. Creating access to drums, a xylophone or even an inexpensive electronic keyboard will increase the chance that such an event will happen again. Music is not only for school, it is for life!

I thank Margarita for allowing me to write this foreword, and it is my sincere wish that you enjoy this book and that you take away ideas you can use with your own children regarding music, regardless of where they go to school.

Please Help Keep Music Alive!

All you need is love,
Louise Harrison

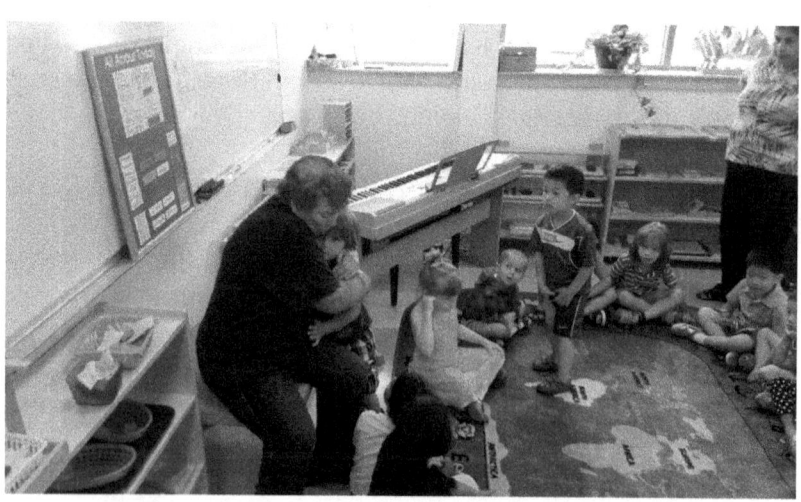

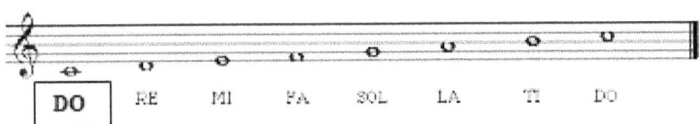

# Chapter One
# The Benefits of Music and Movement

Today we know more about how children learn and grow than ever before. We have data to confirm our hunch that "Music is vital to life." Read what experts in their fields think about the benefits of music and movement:

*"Music brings people together. Through music, children take an inner experience and move it into a shared creative experience. Group music-making releases energy which can be channeled in creative, productive directions. Children learn about themselves and others by playing music together and by listening to each other—tapping into hidden courage that can be played out by singing together or discovering the inner resources to listen quietly to another child's playing."*
**- Judi Bosco**
*Board Certified Music Therapist*

*"Resiliency — to bounce back after a disturbing event is not something we are born with; it must be learned and sometimes that takes many years. There is no vehicle more joyful and playful for providing such training than early childhood music and movement."*
**- Dee Joy Coulter, Ed.D.**
*Neuroscience Educator*

*"A rich voice opens the ear and gives energy to the nervous system. Not only does it help children process and memorize the message, but it also **increases their desire to listen more, learn more, and know more**. A good voice fills the cognitive and emotional brain."*
**- Paul Madaule**
Founder and Director
The Listening Centre

*"Speech and music have a number of shared processing systems. Musical experiences which enhance processing can therefore impact on the perception of language which in turn **impacts on learning to read**."*
**- Susan Hallam**
Institute of Education
University of London

Noted author and neuroscience educator Jane Healy speaks about children whose parents have chosen more "academic" pursuits for their children:
*"Studies show that 4-, 5-, and 6-year-olds in heavily "academic" classes tend to become less creative and more anxious - without gaining significant advantages over their peers."*
**- Jane M. Healy**
Your Child's Growing Mind

*And, if everything else were not convincing enough ... a 2007 poll found that 88% of all post-graduate students in college and 83% of all people earning $150,000 or more had extensive music training.*
**Poll, November 14, 2007**
Reuters, Ltd.

*The Rhythm of Learning*

**Why Music and Movement are Vital for Children:**

Peanut butter and jelly, socks and shoes, bats and balls, hide and seek and music are all elements of childhood. Children are naturally interested in music, and music is naturally good for children. Why is music so attractive to children and why is music so well suited to children?

- Music is a language, and children are oriented toward learning language.
- Music evokes movement, and children delight in and require movement for their development and growth.
- Music engages the brain while stimulating neural pathways associated with such higher forms of intelligence as abstract thinking, empathy, and mathematics.
- Music's melodic and rhythmic patterns provide exercise for the brain and help develop memory. Who among us learned

the ABC's without the ABC song?
- Music is an aural art and young children are aural learners. Since ears are fully mature before birth, infants begin learning from the sounds of their environment before birth.
- Music is perfectly designed for training children's listening skills. Good listening skills and school achievement go hand in hand.
- Developmentally appropriate music activities involve the whole child—the child's desire for language, the body's urge to move, the brain's attention to patterns, the ear's lead in initiating communication, the voice's response to sounds, as well as the eye-hand coordination associated with playing musical instruments.
- Music is a creative experience which involves expression of feelings. Children often do not have the words to express themselves and need positive ways to release their emotions.

- Music transmits culture and is an avenue by which beloved songs, rhymes, and dances can be passed down from one generation to another.

Music is a social activity which involves family and community participation. Children love to sing and dance at home, school, and at church.[1]

It is my strong belief that all children love learning. The very youngest of them soak knowledge up as if they were dry sponges thrown upon the water. At the Montessori schools we also believe that the children learn with their hands. They do an activity with their hands and the muscle memory actually works with the mind memory, enhancing what they learn. So, what we do is show the children how to do something, and then they repeat it with their hands. Let me give you an example as to how I show music to very young children (1 to 6 years of age or even older) …

**Rhythmic flash cards:** I use rhythmic flash cards to help the children develop a sense of how long to hold each type of note. Practicing with these cards also helps to increase the children's memory, attention span and focus when we play a game that involves clapping the rhythm after only looking at the card for a brief moment. We also allow children to improvise their own melodies on top of the rhythms given by these cards. Below is an example of what these cards look like.

www.jaytonmusic.com

I have used my hand-made flash cards with the notes for over 20 years. They are a gigantic size, made out of cardboard and kept in a special order that makes the music easy to learn. I begin with walking out quarter notes. The children step out each beat. It is very simple. The first five flash cards (1-5) are eighth and quarter notes. The next five cards (6-10) introduce the half note, and we actually say them using the eighth and quarter notes as well. When we reach the next five cards (11-15) we introduce the "Rest." We reach the Rest and whisper the word "rest." So, we use the eighth, quarter, and half notes and the Rest in different order. Then I introduce the sixteenth note with clapping and slapping the legs. Yet another set of five cards (16-20) are introduced which are more advanced notes like 16th notes and triplets and even more advanced, and it is a relief to have them all to use during lesson time.

Using the cards five days a week became a challenge for the kids. A seven minute exercise at a music lesson is long and boring if the task is the same every day. So, I came up with a rhythm game. I put five cards down on the floor. I would take one card from the floor, and the kids had to guess which one I had taken out to make the rhythm. (The name of the game is "What Rhythm is Missing?"). The other game, called "Memorize the Rhythm," was introduced as flashcards. After clapping the whole set, I asked children to look at the rhythm card and when I hide it, they will clap without seeing the card, but at the same time memorize the next one. The variation was great, and the children became very proficient. On another day I started to speed up the cards. When I hid a card, they had to look at the next note card and clap it. The next day they used their feet to stamp or run out the varying notes. It was great for motor skills and memory and was fun, fun, fun.

## Naturally musical

In the 15-35 month-old classroom (and with the 3-6 year-olds) music comes naturally. Everyone wants to touch the keys of the piano. Piano time is the most popular work in class. In fact, a piano became the first choice or method to use to adjust children (to calm down the crying child) at the separation/drop-off time in the morning. Just a week ago little 20 months-old Tripp was crying nonstop. The teacher came with him to the office to call the parents. I took Tripp onto my lap, sat with him at the piano and whispered: "let's make a melody for Mommy ..." I showed him two keys around two black keys (E and C) to press with his thumbs. Anybody could do it. I supported those two "sounds" he played with simple chords of tonic, VI chord and IV subdominant. Tripp not only stopped crying ... he magically started to make a nice tune (I quickly managed to video record it). His mom, who almost left in tears herself that morning, was so happy and appreciative.

Curious about how the children were soaking up music, I put a xylophone in the classroom. The same effect occurred. Yes, there could have been disruption in the class because everyone wants to be able to use the instruments. But ... if I bring a drum into class, for example, and show a certain rhythm then the child will learn rather than fighting over the drum and distracting the class. I always have the same cards for a week, so children can practice and later improvise. I must set up a limit time on each instrument, because the young children don't know limits yet ... just like if you set out snacks, they will keep going back to the bowl until it is empty. So, I would put out only five flash cards: then they know they play that rhythm and repeat it or go on to something else. This way it is much easier to redirect to another activity. These children do not sing yet. Given the choice, they will always use the instruments instead. To get past this, I had them begin to sing out their names, ("My name is....that's my name!") and because everyone wanted to be the one to sing their name, they would work hard to follow the melody. Even the youngest, who would use a microphone to amplify her voice, managed to do it. I was so proud of my little ones performance. During the month of January we start to intensively sing with both rooms (toddlers and three to six year-olds). I always include my after-school children. The classes sing two times per day, and I combine older children and toddlers so as to support toddlers voices ... The older kids sing all the toddler's songs to "help them" to finally produce singing voice sounds. I have become very creative in finding simple songs that names different actions children usually do during a day like: "I wake up in the morning early," or "When I wake up in the morning and its quarter to one... you want to have a little fun ... you brush your teeth ... CH-ch-ch-ch (with imitating brushing teeth motion)"or "Big Clock, going tick-tock and tiki-tocki and then the faster ticki-ticki-ticki" or "When Sally puts her ... green ... dress on," and a lot more. I usually change the name and color of the dress/shirt or pants and the motion of the children in order to keep them accurate and present at that time. Then the class responds with a lot of excitement and joy to any music activity we do at that time.

## Hands-on voice training

As I have mentioned, all the material in the classroom is "hands-on" material. The child copies what you do and he learns with his hands. The hand muscle memory is connected to the mind memory. Having a Degree in Music gave me knowledge to teach the hand signs for every piece of music/song the children learned. Using the third and the fifth step I would sing *The Cuckoo Song*, and I would sing their names, and the children would answer by repeating or making their own tune on the third and fifth step. The sixth step was introduced with the song ... *Rain, Rain Go Away*. On the words "Come again aaaaanother day" (we showed the sixth step. The kids became very good at showing the steps with the hand signs.

Introducing the first step did not go as well. I just made up a simple two-step tune on the third and the fifth steps, using the simple words: "We are all driving and then fall down (VVV-I)." On the word "down" it would be a first step with fist falling in child's lap to show the step. And we also learned a second step with the simple tune "Mommy made me mad." The sequence was I-II-III-II-I steps. There are a lot of good songs with a scale melody. Once the class learned "Steps and skips in music" and to voice out the melody, to step up and down singing the C major scale, we began to sing the "This is my school" song. We also made up words to sing the scale songs. For our spring concert children perform the "This is My School" song with hand signs and no accompaniment (a Capella). After the children finish singing a Capella, I check them using a piano key—just to show off to their parents that we did not lose the correct pitch while singing without piano support. Keep in mind that I am talking about 3-5 years old children!

"Hands on" material makes up the majority of material in the classroom. Mathematics, language, sensorial and practical life works (we call it daily living) are easy concepts to understand with concrete materials. I found a great way to teach my class to sing the notes with using hands. This was important as I was limited financially after the break-up with my former partners, and I had left all of my Montessori materials at the school I walked away from. I could not afford to buy expensive Montessori wooden music boards with wooden notes. So, I started to teach my class solfeggio (singing notes) using hand signs. The left hand became a "staff" and the right hand became the pointer, doing finger points into the imaginary line or space on the left hand. I learned this technique from the famous children's composer, George Struve, back in Moscow. It was a surprise how quickly my three-six year-olds began to solfeggio the melody of each song we learned. After a while the children became so proficient, they could learn any melody in a short time. The singing notes skill helped us to impress LOUISE HARRISON, the sister of the famous The Beatles singer George Harrison. I was asked if we could sing any song by George for Louise. It took us less than 20 min to learn with "hands" *Here comes the Sun*, rehearsing and performing this song along with *Yesterday*. Louise loved it! It was a very emotional moment for Louise and all the children. (It also shows how children are naturally very musical.)

*The Rhythm of Learning*

## Dealing with the infamous "I don't want to go to school!" issue

On the second day of school a mom stopped by my office and said, "I'm not sure we're going to sign a contract since we didn't have a great experience yesterday. My daughter doesn't want to be without me, and you don't let parents into the class for a faster adjustment." Being afraid to lose a client I went to one of my teachers and said, "This parent is going to be a volunteer in the class. Please treat her as an assistant, and make sure she is in the classroom for a minimum of two hours." I quickly posted on the board, "If you are interested in volunteering in the class, please sign your name." On the third day of the mother's volunteering the child, Sarah, wasn't following her at all and didn't even notice her disappearance for a while. Problem solved. Like the rest of us, children have some difficulty with change. This doesn't mean they don't want to go to school.

On the fourth day in my Montessori classroom Daniel's mom stopped me in the hallway. She said to me, "My son didn't want to go to school today. He doesn't speak English yet because he just arrived from China." Suspecting this wasn't the real reason for the child's reluctance, I began to ask her questions like: "Why? Was there something else? Was someone not nice to him at school?"

I watched the child in the classroom and he was busy working. He appeared to love the Sport/Gym class, especially when he was catching rings with the sword. Wondering if the problem might lay with his other teacher, I began to feel guilty that I had not done the music class myself the day before. During the work time I was conducting the three period lesson with Sandpaper Letters. And while doing the sandpaper letters on the "T" sound for teacher (we were saying: T-T-T for teacher), he suddenly remarked that "Ms. Teacher never smiles at me."

"At YOU?" I asked.
"No, she doesn't smile at all."
"So you don't like to come to school because you think Ms. Teacher doesn't like you?"
The answer was yes.

Another child named Ivan was saying to his mother: "I don't want to go to school" and, once again, the reality was something completely different (he did not like Nap Time). I am sure many parents have heard, "I don't want to go to school today, my stomach hurts, or I'm sick." The reality is usually something quite different.

When Misha said he didn't want to go to piano lesson and even went so far as to say "I don't like music", it was upsetting for me. I was curious as to why he felt this way, because Misha was very talented and loved piano lessons. After a conversation with his parents, I found out that there was remodeling in the house and that the piano had been moved and was not accessible for practice. Well, guess what? Most children want to be perfect, and if they can't do it well, then they might decide they don't like it!

Another case of not liking going to school or to a piano lesson was the parents complaining of "Paying a lot of money." The reaction of a young child to this is can be, "I don't want to go or I don't like it!" They are just trying to please their parents.

As I've pointed out, incidents such as these are rarely the true reason for the child not wanting to go to school. Ask questions! Investigate.

## What did you do in school today?

Another example of the way children communicate is if you ask your child "What did you do in school today?" They like to say "nothing". But if you ask "Did you do the pink tower today?" they like to say "Yeah!" If you name the activity, there's always a chance to find out what he or she really did. We learn songs in a minimum of 10 languages over the year or even at summer time. We mark on a weekly school calendar the language of the week, so parents may refresh their child's memory as to what they did in school. For our morning line I use a calendar song where we sing the days of the week very softly and sing super loud the actual day of the week. It sounds like: Sunday, Monday, TUESDAY, Wednesday, Thursday, Friday and Saturday. And to help the children remember what they ate for lunch we continue with a Japanese folk tune about "hungry children," naming all the food we ate today and singing backward what we ate the other days of the week. "Today is Tuesday: Tuesday is mashed potatoes; Monday: Monday is macaroni and cheese, all you hungry children come and eat it up, come and eat it up." Music helps children to remember things. So, at the end of each music lesson I make a conclusion by saying "Today we learned a new song in Chinese about a policeman and a boy who found a penny, and we learned a new note D ... etc." Music helps to remember better!

## A drop of water breaks the stone

Getting ready for the end of the year school concert is always frustrating. For example, Sarah and Michael were not here on Tuesdays for the music class. So on the day of the concert I was trying to put them at the end of the line so no one would notice that they hadn't learned the words. The next week I decided to move the class to a different day so more of the class would be in attendance. But for three weeks in a row before the concert some kids were sick—and the concert was again not as successful as I would have liked. Parents wondered why their child was not singing as others.

I was paid for two hours a week for music class. And I was trying to make the practice longer, so that we could repeat all the songs. The challenge was that after a couple lessons some of the children would say, "Ms. Rita is going to make us sing so long." And I had to admit that after thirty minutes everyone seemed to be very exhausted and some of the teachers got frustrated. One of the parents attending was even giving the words so that the children could practice at home to memorize the words.

I used to hear in Russia that a drop of water can break a stone. Using that expression with my friends in America didn't work well at first. "What does it mean that a drop of water can break a stone?" they would ask me. I'd just shrug. When I was in Music College in Russia, the first thing I was taught is that every person will learn to sing well if they can find that balance between hearing and voice. But you have to practice every day. So, in my

*The Rhythm of Learning*

every day line in the class and in my circle time, I took advantage of a piano we had in the classroom. Instead of just doing the line like in a normal Montessori school I was using an instrument so that children would sing with me, and they were hearing the live music while walking, jumping and galloping, etc. At the beginning of the year a child might only be saying the words, not singing at all. But I can remember getting a big surprise when at a meeting with a parent. I was saying, "You know, we will surprise you. If your child sees how other kids sing and you remind him that you want to see him singing (since he has trouble participating in the line) then maybe he will sing." And then the mom said "What? He sings every day, in the shower, in the bathtub, in the car." This was a shock to me. But then I thought about it for a while. Even if the child doesn't participate in the class, he hears (which is part of the Montessori philosophy). A child's brain is like a sponge, so he or she will absorb information like water. As they absorb everything around them collectively, what they learn will come out at some point later, if not in the class. So the winter concert was a big surprise for the mother of the child, and for myself, because the child knew all the words to the songs, and he tried to be in the spotlight.

Having a piano in the classroom opened another advantage. A girl named Melany, after working on the pink tower and some math problems, had begun wandering around trying to get to everyone else's work, her words distracting everybody around. So I took her hand and asked if she wanted to learn how to play Piano, which sparked an interest in her. I showed her just two keys, E and C, and told her to play only those two keys, saying "Let's make a melody!" I played some accompaniment in the bass clef and she started to create her own song. This also got her away from disturbing the other children. The next day, the first thing she did in class was to say she wanted to play piano. So we did three minutes. It became her most desirable "work" to play the piano. I took advantage of her interest by encouraging her to do other work like math first, language second, and then she could play piano. Her parents didn't have a piano at home, and were not interested in signing up for piano lessons because she was only three or they couldn't afford it. When the winter concert came around Santa Claus said "I have one extra present for anyone who will play piano for me." Melany ran first, and I had five piano students at the time who were too shy to go up. But Melany came up and played her easy two note song and made a nice melody. Her mom started crying, and her father ran to me after the concert and asked to sign her up for private lessons, because he thought she had a big talent. Of course every child has the talent.

This goes to show the infiniteness of any child's potential. Dropping a stream of water on a stone may seem meaningless at first—like Melany's two note piano piece. But just as the stone will eventually be eroded over time, so Melany is now capable of playing more complicated pieces.

We were getting ready for the Christmas concert and had watched a snowman movie. A song from the movie, *We are walking in the air*, had everyone humming the tune in the classroom, but the song was outside the range of the children's ability to sing. So I was thinking that it would be hard to include this song into our concert. But the tune was stuck in my head, and I began repeating the lower register of the song. Now, Daniel is one who never gets the tune right, and he actually talked in a low voice. After this particular lesson he said to me, "I want to sing this song as a solo." Knowing that it was not in his range, I told him that when he was singing the song to imagine you are calling your friend who is sitting on the top of a high building. He did this and was suddenly able to squeak out in a super high voice a third octave pitch. At the concert the parents were surprised that Daniel sang in such a beautiful, high tone. Once again, if you just keep doing what you are doing there will always be an amazing result.

## Playing the instruments is the best spent time in the transition (Toddlers) room

Transitions in early childhood programs happen whenever children switch caregivers, move from place to place, or change from one activity to another. For example, children start the day by switching from parent to caregiver, moving from car/bus to inside, and changing from fairly passive sitting to engagement in arrival activities. As necessary and frequent daily experiences, transitions require attention and planning. When transitions are planned as a meaningful part of the curriculum, they promote children's learning, set a positive tone, and help everyone move seamlessly through the day. When transitions are ignored, the results can be unpleasant for children who engage in rowdy or inappropriate behavior and teachers who dread transitions. Transitions that are not carefully and thoughtfully planned compromise children's abilities to benefit from other learning opportunities. What to do?

- Minimize the number of transitions as much as possible. While transitions must occur, young children benefit from a schedule that limits the need to switch too frequently. Too many transitions results in stress for both children and adults. Even when children seem to have had plenty of time to play, it can be difficult for them to leave an activity that has captured their attention and move on simply because "it is time."

- During well-planned transitions, children anticipate and take the lead in doing what is needed to move to the next activity. You support self-management by actively teaching the sequence of activities—what comes first, second, etc.
- Effective teaching allows you to engage children, moving beyond giving orders or needing to constantly tell children what to do next, and enables you to individually support children who may need it.
- Whenever a transition is necessary, it should allow enough time for children to participate at their own pace. Having a transition room where children have the opportunity to play an instrument can be very soothing and even inspirational. It is definitely a time to be enjoyed.[2]

[1]http://www.musikgarten.org/music_movement.com

[2]http://www.ccplus.org/newsletters/17_3.pdf

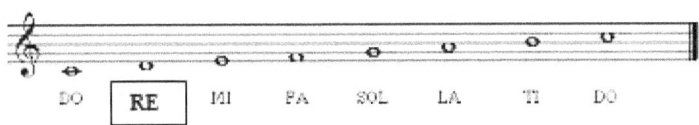

# Chapter Two
# The Montessori Method

**Q. Where did Montessori come from?**
**A.** Montessori (pronounced MON-tuh-SORE-ee) education was founded in 1907 by Dr. Maria Montessori, the first woman in Italy to become a physician. She based her educational methods on scientific observation of children's learning processes. Guided by her discovery that children teach themselves, Dr. Montessori designed a "prepared environment" in which children could freely choose from a number of developmentally appropriate activities. Now, nearly a century after Maria Montessori's first casa dei bambini (children's house) in Rome, Montessori education is found all over the world, spanning ages from birth to adolescence.

**Q. What special training do Montessori teachers have?**
**A.** As with the choice of a Montessori school for children, an adult must also exercise wisdom in choosing a teacher training course. Anyone can legally use the name "Montessori" in describing their teacher training organization. One must be sure the certification earned is recognized by the school where one desires to teach.

The two major organizations offering Montessori training in the United States are the Association Montessori Internationale (AMI, with a U.S. branch office called AMI-USA) and the American Montessori Society (AMS). Most training centers require a bachelor's degree for admission. Training ranges from 200 to 600 pre-service contact hours and covers principles of child development and Montessori philosophy as well as specific uses of the Montessori classroom materials. Montessori training centers can be found across North America and around the world.

There are other courses which can help one better understand Montessori theory or which can train adults to work in certain schools. It is important to balance the amount of time and money one can spend with the teaching opportunities desired.

**Q. What is the difference between Montessori and traditional education?**
**A.** Montessori emphasizes learning through all five senses, not just through listening, watching, or reading. Children in Montessori classes learn at their own, individual pace and according to their own choice of activities from hundreds of possibilities. Learning is an exciting process of discovery leading to concentration, motivation, self-discipline, and a love of learning. Montessori classes place children in three-year age groups (3-6, 6-9, 9-12, and so on), forming communities in which the older children spontaneously share their knowledge with the younger ones. Montessori represents an entirely different approach to education.

**Q. Can I do Montessori at home with my child?**
**A.** Yes, you can use Montessori principles of child development at home. Look at your home through your child's eyes. Children need a sense of belonging, and they get it by participating fully in the routines of everyday life. "Help me do it by myself" is the

life theme of the preschooler. Can you find ways for your child to participate in meal preparation, cleaning, gardening, and caring for clothes and shoes and toys? Providing opportunities for independence is the surest way to build your child's self-esteem.

At the school level many homeschooling and other parents use the Montessori philosophy of following the child's interest and not interrupting concentration to educate their children.

In school only a trained Montessori teacher can properly implement Montessori education, using the specialized learning equipment of the Montessori "prepared environment." Here, social development comes from being in a positive and unique environment with other children—an integral part of Montessori education.

## Montessori Children

**Q. Is Montessori good for children with learning disabilities? What about gifted children?**
**A.** Montessori is designed to help all children reach their fullest potential at their own unique pace. A classroom whose children have varying abilities is a community in which everyone learns from one another and everyone contributes. Moreover, multiage grouping allows each child to find his or her own pace without feeling "ahead" or "behind" in relation to peers.

**Q. What ages does Montessori serve?**
**A.** There are more Montessori programs for ages 3-6 than for any other age group, but Montessori is not limited to early childhood. Many infant/toddler programs (ages 6 months to 3

years) exist, as well as elementary (ages 6-12) classes, adolescent (ages 12-15) groups and even Montessori high schools.

**Q. Are Montessori children successful later in life?**
**A.** Research studies show that Montessori children are well prepared for later life academically, socially, and emotionally. In addition to scoring well on standardized tests, Montessori children are ranked above average on such criteria as following directions, turning in work on time, listening attentively, using basic skills, showing responsibility, asking provocative questions, showing enthusiasm for learning, and adapting to new situations. If the child gets an intensive music exposure at an early age, like before three years-old, he will be much more successful in learning math and reading. Many children in my classroom start reading at three and a half when the statistic shows children start reading at four and a half in a regular Montessori classroom.

**Q. How do I find Montessori schools in my area?**
**A.** There are thousands of Montessori schools in the world, and three "list links" at this site: www.montessori.edu/refs.html. If this doesn't help you, look in your phone book, get the literature of local schools, observe, and compare what you learn this way with what you read on this site. At your first visit you should check if the school is registered with, affiliated with, recognized by or accredited by AMS (American Montessori Society), AMI (American Montessori International), Board of Education or DCFS(Department of Children and Family Services). But the most important observation is in the classroom environment: the happiness of children exuded during the "business" of the child while "working." Only you as a parent will feel the proper energy surrounding your child. The reference list of parents will also help, but keep in mind everyone has a different experience, and you should not expect your child to have same experience as you are told. In our school I always show a very short video

of children working in a classroom, episodes of concerts, but the best is live observation of the classroom and the questions on expectations and concerns that you have as a parent.

**Q. Who accredits or oversees Montessori schools?**
**A.** Unfortunately, there is no way to limit the use of the name "Montessori." Parents must carefully research and observe a classroom in operation in order to choose a real Montessori school for their child.

There are several Montessori organizations to which schools can belong. The two major ones operating in the United States are the Association Montessori Internationale (AMI, with a U.S. branch office called AMI-USA) and the American Montessori Society (AMS). Parents considering placing a child in a Montessori school should ask about the school's affiliation(s).

**Q. How much does Montessori cost?**
**A.** Because all Montessori schools are operated independently of one another, tuitions vary widely. The cost of living in a particular area accounts for the very wide range in tuitions. Median annual tuition by age level will follow. "Median" means that they can be lower and much higher in some places, depending on the cost of living. Montessori schools almost never make a profit and, when compared to the cost-per-child in public schools, are lower.

(NOTE: these figures are several years old and may not apply today.)

- Infant/toddler: $4,200+
- Ages 3-6, 3-hour day: $3,850+
- Ages 3-6, 4-hour day: $4,500+
- Ages 3-6, 6-hour day: $5,875+
- Ages 6-9: $6,690

- Ages 9-12: $6,700+
- Ages 12-15 and 15-18: $8,170+

Also keep in mind that there are many Montessori programs in public schools, which charge no tuition at all to students within their district. The most important question is: What will your child's education include for this price: work time, music lessons (how many times a week), gymnastics or gym class, what meal is included or not and what extracurricular classes your child can get on or off site?

**Q. What is the best way to choose a Montessori school for my child?**
A. Ask if the school is affiliated with any Montessori organization. Ask what kind of training the teachers have. Visit the school, observe the classroom in action, and later ask the teacher or principal to explain the theory behind the activities you saw. Most of all, talk to your child's prospective teacher about his or her philosophy of child development and education to see if it is compatible with your own.

**Q. How many Montessori schools are there?**
A. Estimates are that there are at least 4,000 certified Montessori schools in the United States and about 7,000 worldwide.

**Q. Are Montessori schools religious?**
A. Some are, but most are not. Some Montessori schools, just like other schools, operate under the auspices of a church, synagogue, or diocese, but most are independent of any religious affiliation.

**Q. Are all Montessori schools private?**
A. No. Approximately 200 public schools in the U.S. and Canada offer Montessori programs, and this number is growing every year.

*The Rhythm of Learning*

**Q. What does it take to start a Montessori school?**
**A.** The essential element of any Montessori school is the fully-trained Montessori teacher. A good starting point is a group of parents who want Montessori for their children. The next step is to look into state and local requirements for schools, such as teacher training, facilities, class size, etc. Selecting a site and making sure it meets applicable building codes is also an early part of the process. Montessori materials and furniture must be purchased, and, unless one of the founders has taken Montessori training, a teacher must be hired.

## Some Specific Details of the Montessori Method

### The schedule: The three-hour work period
Under the age of six, there are one or two 3-hour, uninterrupted work periods each day, not broken up by required group lessons. Older children schedule meetings or study groups with each other or the teacher when necessary. Adults and children respect concentration and do not interrupt someone who is busy at a task. Groups form spontaneously or are arranged ahead by special appointment. They almost never take precedence over self-selected work.

### Multi-age grouping
Children are grouped in mixed ages and abilities in three to six year spans: 0-3, 3-6, 6-12 (sometimes temporarily 6-9 and 9-12), 12-15, 15-18. There is constant interaction, problem solving, child to child teaching, and socialization. Children are challenged according to their ability and are never bored. The Montessori

middle and high school teacher ideally has taken all three training courses plus graduate work in an academic area or areas.

### Work centers
The environment is arranged according to subject area, and children are always free to move around the room instead of staying at desks. There is no limit to how long a child can work with a piece of material. At any one time in a day all subjects: math, language, science, history, geography, art, music, etc., will be being studied, at all levels.

### Teaching method ... "Teach by teaching, not by correcting"
There are no papers turned back with red marks and corrections. Instead the child's effort and work is respected as it is. The teacher, through extensive observation and record-keeping, plans individual projects to enable each child to learn what he needs in order to improve.

### Teaching Ratio - 1:1 and 1:30+
Except for infant/toddler groups (Ratio is dictated by local social service regulations), the teaching ratio is one trained Montessori teacher and one non-teaching aide to 30+ children. Rather than lecturing to large or small groups of children, the teacher is trained to teach one child at a time, and to oversee thirty or more children working on a broad array of tasks. She is facile in the basic lessons of math, language, the arts and sciences, and in guiding a child's research and exploration, capitalizing on his interest in and excitement about a subject. The teacher does not make assignments or dictate what to study or read, nor does she set a limit as to how far a child follows an interest.

### Basic lessons
The Montessori teacher spends a lot of time during teacher training practicing the many lessons with materials in all areas.

She must pass a written and oral exam on these lessons in order to be certified. She is trained to recognize a child's readiness according to age, ability, and interest in a specific lesson, and is prepared to guide individual progress.

**Areas of study**
All subjects are interwoven, not taught in isolation, the teacher modeling a "Renaissance" person of broad interests for the children. A child can work on any material he understands at any time.

**Class size**
Except for infant/toddler groups, the most successful classes are of 30-35 children to one teacher (who is very well trained for the level she is teaching), with one or two non-teaching assistants. This is possible because the children stay in the same group for three to six years and much of the teaching comes from the children and the environment.

**Learning styles**
All kinds of intelligences and styles of learning are nurtured: musical, bodily-kinesthetic, spatial, interpersonal, intrapersonal, intuitive, and the traditional linguistic and logical-mathematical (reading, writing, and math). This particular model is backed up by Harvard psychologist Howard Gardner's theory of multiple intelligences.

**Assessment**
There are no grades or other forms of reward or punishment, subtle or overt. Assessment is by portfolio and the teacher's observation and record keeping. The test of whether or not the system is working lies in the accomplishment and behavior of the children, their happiness, maturity, kindness, and love of learning and level of work.

**Requirements for ages 0-6**
There are no academic requirements for this age, but children are exposed to amazing amounts of knowledge and often learn to read, write and calculate beyond what is usually thought interesting to a child of this age.

**Requirements for ages 6-18**
The teacher remains alert to the interests of each child and facilitates individual research in following interests. There are no curriculum requirements except those set by the state, or college entrance requirements, for specific grade levels. These take a minimum amount of time. From age six on, students design contracts with the teacher to guide their required work, to balance their general work, and to teach them to become responsible for their own time management and education. The work of the 6+ class includes subjects usually not introduced until high school or college.

**Character education:**
Education of character is considered equally with academic education, children learning to take care of themselves, their environment, each other, cooking, cleaning, building, gardening, moving gracefully, speaking politely, being considerate and helpful, doing social work in the community, etc.

## Montessori Teachers

**Q. What special training do Montessori teachers have?**
**A.** As with the choice of a Montessori school for children, an adult must also exercise wisdom in choosing a teacher training

course. Anyone can legally use the name "Montessori" in describing their teacher training organization. One must be sure the certification earned is recognized by the school where one desires to teach.

The two major organizations offering Montessori training in the United States are the Association Montessori International (AMI, with a U.S. branch office called AMI-USA) and the American Montessori Society (AMS). Most training centers require a bachelor's degree for admission. Training ranges from 200 to 600 pre-service contact hours and covers principles of child development and Montessori philosophy as well as specific uses of the Montessori classroom materials. Montessori training centers can be found across North America and around the world.

There are other courses which can help one better understand Montessori theory or which can train adults to work in certain schools. It is important to balance the amount of time and money one can spend with the teaching opportunities desired.

## Montessori Materials

**Q. What materials are used?**
A. It is the philosophy and the knowledge of the teacher that is essential in the success of a Montessori class.
One must be wary of the use of the words "Montessori materials" as many people today use the words as a selling point for materials that have no use in the Montessori classroom and that can be distracting and impede a child's progress.

The "sensorial," math, and some of the language and cultural materials (metal insets, sandpaper letters, puzzle maps, bells, for example) are professionally manufactured according to traditional standards that have been tested over many years. However, even some of these are made by newer companies that do not fully understand the reason for certain details and so produce materials that are not as successful. There is a "materials committee" in Holland that oversees the quality of materials used in AMI (Association Montessori Internationale) schools, for example.

Montessori teachers, for very good reasons, make many of their own practical life and language materials instead of buying them, as they learn to do in their training, depending on where in the world they live. They gather practical life materials piece by piece. This is an important process that gives a unique quality to each classroom that expresses the culture and ideas of beauty in each community—instead of all classrooms looking alike with no personal touches. Materials in the classroom, without being used correctly by a trained teacher, are usually worthless in creating a real Montessori class, but they can help in some ways in non-Montessori situations. For example, the math materials have been used to teach a concept sensorially thus helping a child to make the abstraction. Educational materials in the Montessori method serve a very different purpose than in traditional education where the text books are ordered and the teacher learns how to use them. This difference is because in Montessori the child learns from the environment, and it is the teacher's job to put the child in touch with the environment, not to "teach" the child. Thus the creation of the environment, and selection of materials is done mostly by the teacher and is very important.

In Montessori education having too many materials is often worse than not having enough. In this country (USA) there are

*The Rhythm of Learning*

many materials suppliers, unfortunately, who are not Montessori trained and do not understand the purpose of materials, and who sell items that scatter the child's energy, or waste time, clutter the environment, etc. It is very important to choose carefully when selecting materials for using the Montessori method of education in school or in the home.

In a Montessori school, unlike in a daycare, the child is entered into a learning program, one that believes the child, regardless of the age, is ready to soak up whatever you are willing to show him or her.

As with all my students, relative **Solfeggio** with the **Kodály** method is used to teach children pitch and sight singing.

Solfeggio is the ABC's of music. It teaches you pitch, to hear and sing harmonies, and how to write down the music you create in your head.

What is **Solfeggio**? It describes the musical scale using one-vowel-sound syllables that sing easier than the traditional 8-note scale names: C-D-E-F-G-A-B-C or scale numbers: 1-2-3-4-5-6-7-1.

The Solfeggio scale looks like this: Do-Re-Mi-Fa-Sol-La-Ti-Do. Solfeggio is not only easier to sing, but simplifies music and works with complicated scores as well. For instance, I just described a C-Major scale, but solfeggio also describes minor and non-traditional scales, too.

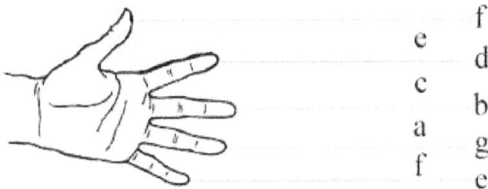

**Synonyms and Pronunciation:** "Solfeggio" is a French term. Solmization describes the act of singing something in solfeggio or any other system using syllables to describe a musical scale.

**Why Learn Solfeggio?** With solfeggio you learn songs quickly and well. It helps you sight-sing or learn music without hearing a tune played first. Solmization increases sight-singing skills by revealing patterns in music. Instead of seeing two random notes in a piece of music, you recognize those two notes as something you have sung before.

Solfeggio basically takes the very complicated system of 12 major keys and combines it into one. Without solfeggio you might sing 100 songs and still take hours to learn a new one. Solfeggio also improves your ability to sing particular intervals (the space between notes), which improves your overall pitch. In my school/class we sing notes EVERY DAY. It can be a scale or melody line from a song we are working on. It does not have to be perfect, but it is important for children to visualize where the melody goes, where the repeats, steps, skips, etc. are. Since we solfeggio every day, my young children are capable of learning and memorizing very advanced songs in a very short time.

**ABC's of Music?** When you first learn to read, you learn your ABC's. The solfeggio syllables (Do-Re-Mi-Fa-Sol-La-Ti-Do) are just that. As you know, if all you can do is recite your ABC's, then you have not learned to read yet. To take the metaphor a bit further, reading a book is the equivalent to being able to sight-sing.

The **Kodály Method**, also referred to as the **Kodály Concept**, is an approach to music education developed in Hungary during the mid-twentieth century by Zoltán Kodály. His philosophy of education served as inspiration for the method, which was then developed over a number of years by his associates.

Kodály became interested in the music education of children in 1925 when he overheard some students singing songs that they had learned at school. Kodály was appalled by the standard of the children's singing, and was inspired to do something to improve the music education system in Hungary. He wrote a number of controversial articles, columns, and essays to raise awareness about the issue of music education. In his writings, Kodály criticized schools for using poor-quality music and for only teaching music in the secondary grades. Kodály insisted that the music education system needed better teachers, better curriculum, and more class time devoted to music.

Beginning in 1935, along with his colleague Jenő Ádám, he embarked on a long-term project to reform music teaching in the lower and middle schools by actively creating a new curriculum and new teaching methods, as well as writing new musical compositions for children. His work resulted in the publication of several highly influential books that have had a profound impact on musical education both inside and outside his home country.

Kodály's efforts finally bore fruit in 1945 when the new Hungarian government began to implement his ideas in the public schools. Socialist control of the educational system facilitated the establishment of Kodály's methods nationwide. The first music primary school, in which music was taught daily, opened in 1950. The school was so successful that over one hundred music primary schools opened within the next decade. After about fifteen years roughly half the schools in Hungary were music schools.

Kodály's success eventually spilled outside of Hungarian borders. Kodály's method was first presented to the international community in 1958 at a conference of the International Society for Music Educators (I.S.M.E.) held in Vienna. Another I.S.M.E. conference in Budapest in 1964 allowed participants to see Kodály's work first-hand, causing a surge of interest. Music educators from all over the world traveled to Hungary to visit Kodály's music schools. The first symposium dedicated solely to the Kodály method was held in Oakland, California in 1973; it was at this event that the International Kodály Society was inaugurated. Today Kodály-based methods are used throughout the world.

**Pedagogy**
Using these principles as a foundation, Kodály's colleagues, friends, and most talented students developed the actual pedagogy now called the Kodály Method. Many of the techniques used were adapted from existing methods. The creators of the Kodály Method researched music educational techniques used throughout the world and incorporated those they felt were the best and most suited for use in Hungary.

**Child-developmental approach**
Kodály Method uses a child-developmental approach to sequence, introducing skills according to the capabilities of the child. New concepts are introduced beginning with what is easiest for the child and progressing to the more difficult. Children are first introduced to musical concepts through experiences such as listening, singing, or movement. It is only after the child becomes familiar with a concept that he or she learns how to notate it, similar to methods like Suzuki and Simply Music. Concepts are constantly reviewed and reinforced through games, movement, songs, and exercises.

*The Rhythm of Learning*

**Rhythm syllables**
The Kodály Method incorporates rhythm syllables similar to those created by nineteenth-century French theoretician Emile-Joseph Chêvé. In this system, note values are assigned specific syllables that express their durations. For example, quarter notes are expressed by the syllable *ta* while eighth note pairs are expressed using the syllables *ti-ti*. Larger note values are expressed by extending ta to become *ta-a* or *ta-o* (half note), ta-a-a or ta-o-o (dotted half note), and *ta-a-a-a* or ta-o-o-o (whole note). These syllables are then used when sight-reading or otherwise performing rhythms. My Transition Room children with age of 15 months and older very confidently respond with clapping and naming the rhythm notes as ta for quarter, ta-ah for half notes with a 1-2 count, ta-o-o-o for whole notes on a 1-2-3-4 count. They love to use sticks for performing simple melody rhythms. Back in Russia this method was used in public schools for seven years-old and up. But, once I simplified the cards, made them a bigger size and (most importantly) repeated the same cards over and over with clapping and playing percussions (over a period of three months) it got into my toddlers physiology, and playing sticks with piano became an everyday activity which we are mastering each day better and better.

**Rhythm and movement**
The Kodály Method also includes the use of rhythmic movement, a technique inspired by the work of Swiss music educator Emile Jaques-Dalcroze. Kodály was familiar with Dalcroze's techniques and agreed that movement is an important tool for the internalization of rhythm. To reinforce new rhythmic concepts, the Kodály Method uses a variety of rhythmic movements, such as walking, running, marching, and clapping. These may be performed while listening to music or singing. Some singing exercises call for the teacher to invent appropriate rhythmic movements to accompany the songs.

## Rhythm sequence and notation

Rhythmic concepts are introduced in a child-developmentally appropriate manner based upon the rhythmic patterns of their folk music (for example, 6/8 is more common in English than 2/4 so it should be introduced first). The first rhythmic values taught are quarter notes and eighth notes, which are familiar to children as the rhythms of their own walking and running. Rhythms are first experienced by listening, speaking in rhythm syllables, singing, and performing various kinds of rhythmic movement. Only after students internalize these rhythms is notation introduced. The Kodály Method uses a simplified method of rhythmic notation, writing note heads only when necessary, such as for half notes and whole notes.

## Movable-do solfege

The Kodály Method uses a system of movable-do solfege syllables, in which, during sight-singing, scale degrees are sung using corresponding syllable names (*do, re, mi, fa, sol, la,* and *ti*). The syllables show function within the key and the relationships between pitches, not absolute pitch. Kodály was first exposed to this technique while visiting England, where a movable-do system created by Sarah Glover and augmented by John Curwen was being used nationwide as a part of choral training. Kodály found movable-do solfege to be helpful in developing a sense of tonal function, thus improving students' sight-singing abilities. Kodály felt that movable-do solfege should precede acquaintance with the staff, and developed a type of shorthand using solfege initials with simplified rhythmic notation.

## Melodic sequence and pentatony

Scale degrees are introduced in accordance with child-developmental patterns. The first Kodály exercise books were based on the diatonic scale, but educators soon found that children struggled to sing half steps in tune and to navigate within such a wide range. Thus the pentatonic scale came to be used as a sort of stepping stone. Revised Kodály exercises begin with the minor third (*so-mi*) and then, one at a time, add *la, do,* and *re*. Only after children become comfortable with these pitches are *fa* and *ti* introduced, a much simpler feat when taught in relation to the already established pentatonic scale. Kodály stated that each nation should create its own melodic sequence based upon its own folk music.

**Hand signs**
Depiction (left) of Curwen's Solfege hand signs. This version includes the tonal tendencies and interesting titles for each tone. Hand signs, also borrowed from the teachings of Curwen, are performed during singing exercises to provide a visual aid. This technique assigns to each scale degree a hand sign that shows its particular tonal function. For example, *do, mi,* and *so* are stable in appearance, whereas *fa* and *ti* point in the direction of *mi* and *do*, respectively. Likewise, the hand sign for *re* suggests motion to do, and that of *la* to *so*. Kodály added to Curwen's hand signs upward/downward movement, allowing children to actually see the height or depth of the pitch. The signs are made in front of the body, with *do* falling about at waist level and *la* at eye level. Their distance in space corresponds with the size of the interval they represent. The hand signs were featured in the 1977 film, *Close Encounters of the Third Kind*.

**Materials**
Kodály Method materials are drawn strictly from two sources: "authentic" folk music and "good-quality" composed music. Folk music was thought to be an ideal vehicle for early musical training because of its short forms, pentatonic style, and simple language. Of the classical repertoire, elementary students sing works of major composers of the Baroque, Classical, and Romantic music eras, while secondary-level students sing music from the twentieth century as well.

Kodály collected, composed, and arranged a large number of works for pedagogical use. Along with Béla Bartók and other associates, Kodály collected and published six volumes of Hungarian folk music, including over one thousand children's songs. Much of this literature was used in Kodály Method song books and textbooks. High quality music was needed in short and simple forms in order to bridge the gap between folk music and classical works. For this purpose, Kodály composed thousands of songs and sight-singing exercises, making up sixteen educational publications, six of which contain multiple volumes of over one hundred exercises each. Kodály's complete pedagogical works are published collectively by Boosey & Hawkes as *The Kodály Choral Method*.

**Results**
Studies have shown that the Kodály Method improves intonation, rhythm skills, music literacy, and the ability to sing in increasingly complex parts. Outside of music, it has been shown to improve perceptual functioning, concept formation, motor skills, and performance in other academic areas such as reading and math.[3]

**Hand Signs**
There are signs you can make with your hands associated with each solfeggio syllable. For some it is an added complication and for others, like me, it helps you recall syllables quickly. If you lean towards a kinesthetic or visual learning style, I highly recommend learning them.

**Moveable-Do**
There are two solfeggio practices: "moveable-do" and "fixed-do." Moveable-do combines all 12 keys into one, and fixed-do does not. How? No matter what musical key you are in "do" always starts on the first scale note. So, C is "do" in C-major, G is "do" in G-major, D is "do" in D-major, and etc. Solfeggio

reveals that no matter what key all major scales are the same; the only difference is the pitch you start on. Most schools and universities in English speaking countries teach moveable-do.

**Is That It?**
No! There are other syllables to learn and much more. If you sing a chromatic scale up, the syllables are: do-di-re-ri-mi-fa-fi-sol-si-la-li-ti-do. Going down, the syllables change to: do-ti-te-la-le-sol-se-fa-mi-me-re-ra-do. The system is genius, but to understand why the syllables change going up and down is complex. As a beginner, you should just be aware there is more to it and start simple.

Many music education methods use solfeggio to teach pitch and sight-reading, most notably the Kodály Method.

The study of solfeggio enables the musician to audiate, or mentally hear, the pitches of a piece of music which he or she is seeing for the first time and then to sing them aloud. Solfeggio study also improves recognition of musical intervals (perfect fifths, minor sixths, etc.), and strengthens the understanding of music theory. Solfeggio is a form of solmization and the two terms are sometimes used interchangeably.

The technique of solfeggio involves assigning the notes of a scale a particular syllable, and then practicing by singing different note sequences using these syllables. The sequences gradually get more difficult in terms of intervals and rhythms used.

The seven syllables commonly used for this practice in English-speaking countries are: *do, re, mi, fa, sol, la* and *ti*.

There are two ways of applying solfeggio: 1) fixed "do", where the syllables are always tied to specific pitches (e.g. "do" is always the pitch "C") and 2) movable "do," where the syllables are assigned to different pitches based on musical context.[4]

All this may seem complicated, but the work is shown bit by bit, and using **Choir Solfeggio** we manage to teach children to remember over 20 melodies a year.

**Choir Solfeggio: The Note's House**
I always forget that the children at my school are so young. The song *This is My School* has been sung at the concerts many times. Parents always love to see the hand signs shown by the children when they sing. We can sing real notes I told my current children. All the notes live in an imaginary house (the staff). The note C (do) lives in the basement on what is called the ledger line. The rest of the notes live on the lines or the spaces or on the steps used in the hand signs. By the next concert we were showing the notes with the hand signs and singing the notes, instead of using the steps. It was a big success.

**Backwards Singing**
In order to help children remember the words to our songs I will practice singing it backwards with them. For example if I wanted them to remember *the Itsy bitsy spider...*

Original: The "itsy" backwards practice with children singing ...

spout
Water spout
The water spout
Up the water spout
Went up the water spout
Spider went up the water spout
Bitsy spider went up the water spout
Itsy bitsy spider went up the water spout
The itsy bitsy spider went up the water spout

*The Rhythm of Learning*

## Introduction to composition

Making melody starts from the very first music lesson at the beginning of the school year. I start a conversation with the kids: this is a music lesson, which means that we will be singing most of the time, playing, performing by clapping, or playing an instrument, etc. ... not much talking. So, instead of asking your name or telling you mine, I will sing my question to you. Example: What's your name? And you will need to sing your name to me. I sing my motive using fifth and third steps (like a Coo-coo songJ):"What's your name?"...The answer follows:"My name is ...Rita" ...I sing-ask to every child in my classroom group using 5th and 3d or 5th and 1st steps-degrees of the major scale using hand signs (any music or Montessori teacher knows how to do it). After 5 times singing it, I change the pitch to higher or lower, in the stepping or skipping notes melodies. Children pick up quickly and some begin improvising. FOR LATER LESSONS I MAY CHANGE MY QUESTION TO: how are you?, or what did you eat?, How did you sleep?, Are you happy? (the answer will be: Yes I am, or "No I don't"(Never had that one) etc... Later, when children learn stepping or skipping up or down notes with different intervals I give them example: if I sing my tune stepping up, you may sing back to me stepping down, any opposites or ...Let's make your own song!

Children can start making their own music using The Rhythm cards in the class during work time. Each card has 4 beats in it and usually a child picks up several cards at a time (from set of two to six cards). After mastering the Rhythm of each card by clapping same card several times, the child starts mixing them up, placing them on their work rug in different order and wile clapping, he/she realize the rhythm pattern is very different each time they change the order of cards.Some children clapped the cards in different order. For example Jonny would always start with quarter notes and Masha would pick eighth notes only. Then they would mix the cards and play the rhythm with rhythm sticks or other percussion instruments (in a certain order). Then one child began to play the rhythm on the triangle. I put two cards on the piano and the next student followed the rhythm on the piano. The next student tried to pick several cards and made his own rhythm. I provided paper, and then the students began to write down their own tunes. I provided the music staff paper and Jonny wrote his own notes. Younger Masha would copy or trace and then write-draw her "very own note's signs" on white paper and me and her were so proud of her achievement! This was done all on their own, with me just providing the opportunity. It was amazing to watch my three to six year-old children making their own tunes on the piano or the keyboard. Before I introduced keyboard in the class, I set up a simple rule: ONE finger at a time, and ONE key at a time are all that will be allowed to be used and played. It is fun to watch how a child focuses while making a motive, tune, or melody ... with no banging on the piano.

[4]Wikipedia

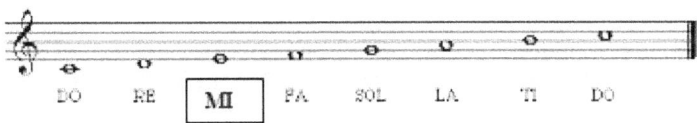

# Chapter 3
# My Journey

My torn piano book flew out of the window.

"Next time you won't make mistakes!" barked my piano teacher.

I walked downstairs, barely holding in my tears. I was thinking, "I never will come back for another piano lesson."

These are the only memories I have of my first piano teacher—other than the time, I was playing Czerny Etude.

I wanted to learn to play the piano so badly. At ballet class, I followed the concertmaster all the time. I loved watching her fingers flying over the keyboard. She's the one who told my mom to take me to music school. But I was not accepted because my hands were just not right for piano-playing. However, when I was in third grade I again received the piano concertmaster's recommendation, and this time I was accepted. I practiced and performed with other third and fourth-grade music students.

In retrospect, one proud, memorable moment was when I performed a piano concerto with the orchestra. The composer who wrote the concerto was very famous in our city. In light of that, I remember my fear of being on stage and all of the possible mistakes I could make. My trembling fingers slipped off the keys several times, but nobody noticed. By the end of my performance loud applause filled the music hall. In response, I bowed several times, smiling at the audience. It was truly a moment of triumph for me, but the best feeling was knowing how proud my father was, that I performed the concerto with grace and that I was the youngest performer in a concert where many dignitaries had decided to attend.

Despite my outstanding performance, I was afraid to tell my mom that I no longer wanted to attend piano lessons, that I hated my music teacher. I knew she invested a large amount of money in me to train. Her average salary was about 80 rubles a month and the tuition for one month of music school cost 24 rubles. Times were rough. Mulling over my conflicted heart, I didn't sleep all night. But the next morning, my mom and I were called to music school. My piano teacher was moving to a different town, meaning I could choose any piano teacher in the whole school! I chose Vassa Vasilievna. I don't know why I selected her, but she had two daughters with the most beautiful reddish-golden hair. Just like them, I had long hair, but I wished it was the same color as theirs.

I enjoyed the last four years of music school. It was during this time that I was the happiest, the most satisfied. Vassa was a tactful teacher; firm but respectful. She seldom raised her voice, and she showed the best exercises and tricks for sharpening my piano techniques. She even owned a house (in Russia it's very rare to have your own house. You are expected to pay for it with your own money, as no home loans are available). I loved going to Vassa's house for extra practice. She became part of my family. I also learned to love performing in concerts.

*The Rhythm of Learning*

After high school I wanted to go into theatre, but my mom wouldn't allow me to leave the town; she despised acting. But I did have the choice to either receive a Bachelor's (or a Master's) degree in teaching or to attend the music college.

Our music college in Bryansk was a very prestigious school. I decided to major in choir conducting. After graduating this would allow me to have more of a variety of teaching positions, especially those geared toward music, like teaching piano, music theory and choir conducting. To declare this major was a competitive process. In order to be accepted to this college students were supposed to take piano, dictation, sight reading and academics exams. Only 30 students out of 1500 applicants were accepted. And I was one of them.

We started with 30 students but by graduation, the number dwindled down to 13 students who received diplomas. I still admire how we were able to manage such a busy schedule. We had to divvy up our time between five hours of academics, two private piano lessons, two music theory classes, reading music literature, two choir group lessons, and practicing piano for two hours a day. I would wake up and practice from 6 to 8 a.m. so I could make it to my classes which started at 9 a.m.

I lived on the second-floor in a five-story building. When I played piano, my neighbors, who were sweet old ladies, could hear me. They always sat on the bench by the entrance to the building and knew everything about everybody in the neighborhood. Once, they mentioned to my mom how good I played, to which she answered, "Yeah, Rita will play for hours instead of washing dishes!"

When Vassa found out that I did not pursue a major in piano performance, she was upset and didn't want to talk to me anymore. I knew that one day I would play so well that she would be proud of me anyway. Her approval meant a lot.

For my final exam in choir conducting my teacher gave me **An American Folk Song** to conduct with the college choir. That was the first sign of America coming to me. I had an outstanding success with this song and got the highest grade.

July 10th was the date of my technology test. If I didn't pass this exam, I would not receive my diploma. I did not mention I was 9 months pregnant. I went to take my test with dull pain. Somehow, I passed the exam. My son was born shortly after.

I was supposed to have an interview the next day for a job at a boarding school. *The only one position open for a music teacher in Bryansk.* The government was sending college graduates to faraway places in deep countries and villages like in Siberia, Chukotka, and Dagestan—just not the main cities, though. They wanted more people working in smaller villages to raise education standards of the country.

What could I do? I was lucky enough to even get an interview, which I got because I was the only student with all A's out of the 13 remaining graduates of the class.

The principle of the boarding school welcomed me, letting me know that "Last year, dear, we had three teachers quit due to the disciplinary challenges in their classes. One ended up in the hospital. While we see that you have great potential, you need to be strong and to be open to challenges in the behavior of the students. Most of them are from very bad families."

"No problem," I replied crisply, "I know that the kids will love me."

*The Rhythm of Learning*

I was confident because I didn't have a choice.

Working at the boarding school was (as promised) very challenging, but it was also a lot of fun, and I had a great relationship with the kids. I would always be telling them stories about classical, romantic, and baroque composers. We even sang "Yesterday" by the Beatles (I guess it was a second sign of America).

When I was in my third year of Music College, I started taking parallel credit hours in Pedagogical University of Academic Petrovsky in Psychology and with a Methods of Primary Education major. The classes in university had been great, and I loved learning how to teach elementary-age art, gym, and math classes. But I realized that it was not a Master's degree in music. If I didn't try this coming summer to pass professional music exams, I would lose my credentials. I was worried that I would not be qualified, especially in music dictation. Luckily, I had my red diploma from Music College. I had it right in my hands and that's what I brought to the Moscow Pedagogical Institute. It earned me the chance to try to pass the exams. This time it was more competitive than at Bryansk College.

That was the year when Vladimir Visotsky died and when the Olympics were held in Moscow. Such great, amazing people I met there. Best of all, it was the year I met my forever girlfriend, Tanya, from Kursk. We had a connection at first sight. She's the only person who could keep up with my quick thoughts and, from one glance, understand what I meant without me even saying it. If my Latvian teacher said something super funny in choir class, we could look at each other and laugh or try not to laugh at the same time. No explanations ever needed and no arguments ever happened, except for one time, when she was waiting for me at the train station. We didn't have cell phones to communicate and thinking she might have left on the train for home, I boarded the train, leaving her to look for me at the train station for a few hours. I felt guilty afterward, but we laughed it off and made amends.

Studying at the Moscow Institute was insanely difficult. My day would start at 5:30 a.m. I would take the earliest train as soon as the METRO train station was open. Tanya and I would arrive at the Institute at 6 a.m. and grab a room with a piano, because if we didn't, there would be no more instruments to practice. We would take a short nap right on the closed lid of the piano for an extra half-hour and resume practicing until 9 a.m., the start of our first class. We loved hanging out in the small park at the front of the building, smoking with the teachers and talking about everything; young composers, new poets, new music, new movies, new operas or plays in the theaters ... the list was endless.

The schedule of classes ran much the same way as in the Music College in Bryansk. From 9 a.m. to 12 p.m. we had three classes that included: Modern Russian Language, Dialectic or Historical Materialism, Scientific Communism, Political Economy, Marksizm-Leninizm, Philosophy, etc.. The idea was that you could not be a good musician if you were not politically stable or educated.

The first and second years were crazy since I was attending the same classes at the Bryansk Pedagogical Institute. The freedom came in my third year when I graduated successfully from the Bryansk Pedagogical Institute of G. Petrovski with a major in Psychology and Elementary Education. Happily I brought my diploma to the office of the Moscow Institute, asking for permission to not attend the political classes anymore since I already finished them and had the credits to show for it. But what I was told was that if I did not bring the approval from the

*The Rhythm of Learning*

Moscow Board of Education, I could be sued by the government (education in Russia was free that time) for the overuse of funds for education in the Soviet Union!

I ran to the Board of Education and asked for an appointment with the secretary of the Minister of Education. I submitted all my grades and evaluation reports for every class I attended in Bryansk, indicating that I had good grades in every subject. Finally, they gave me a letter that allowed me to drop all of the political classes. That bought me three more hours for extra piano practice, voice lessons, or just for my leisure.

I had two extraordinary, exciting years of learning, going to theaters, and famous performances with no politics involved. I was blessed to be noticed by the great talented children's composer, Georgiy Alexandrovich Struve. In Music College, we studied all of the music manuals, which were considered as "Bibles" for good music teachers. We thought of Alexander Sokolov, Georgiy Struve, Dimitri Kabalevsky, Shnitke, Pakhmutova as gods of music. We college students admired and studied their music religiously.

When I met Georgiy Struve, I learned that he had a very poor life. He wrote music for movies, barely enough for bread and butter. Struve gave me tickets to Bolshoi theater, the theatre on Taganka (where Visotsky played when he was alive), the theater of Dolls, the theater of Satira (comedy theater), and the theater of Operetta. Poor students could never afford even the cheapest tickets to these theaters. You couldn't buy the tickets anyway in the Soviet Union. Everything was black market only.

During my last year at the Moscow Pedagogical Institute Tanya and I couldn't afford to make the rent. Struve generously helped me get a room at the international hotel "Druzhba" (friendship). I didn't see the benefits of this hotel. I would leave every morning at 5:30 a.m. and come back at 10 or 11 p.m. But my classmates knew it was a great hotel and wanted to celebrate the end of session there. We were residents of the hotel and had access to restaurants and ballrooms.

But life and my problems went on. I worked at seven different jobs at the time. I was a substitute elementary teacher, I worked as a full-time music teacher at the boarding school, and I worked part-time as a teacher at the Music College. For three hours a week I worked at the Pedagogical Institute, teaching methods of music education to music teachers. I also worked teaching piano at a private music school and at home. Also, every Sunday morning, I had two hours of folklore choir practice at the Center of Music.

After much thought I decided there were better opportunities for me in America.

I worked hard to get my stamped visa and, soon enough, I had my flight to the United States all booked. I settled in Chicago in a one-bedroom apartment on Kenmore Avenue. I loved the short walk to Lake Michigan and the stores around the area.

My adaptation to America wasn't what I thought it would be. The kinds of residents of the building in which I lived were varied. You'd get the local thief, who was actually a very nice and helpful neighbor from Moscow, to a very well-educated engineer, also hailing from the Soviet Union.

I worked as a babysitter from Monday to Friday from 8 a.m. to 5 p.m. They had a grand piano, so when kids were sleeping, I would softly practice.

At a party in a Russian restaurant one lady who worked as a dental assistant and was a former Russian musician told me that she saw an advertisement on a position in the Elk Grove Park District as a piano teacher. She gave me the number but advised me to not give out references. I wrote a short biography for myself using the dictionary. When I called the manager, I was told that position was filled. They no longer needed anybody.

"Why did you say no if you didn't even see me?" I said.

The lady on the other end laughed and gave me the address and a time for an interview. I was afraid that they wouldn't understand me. The director of the school district explained that they didn't need a piano teacher, but if I offered a program for a younger age, they would be open to reconsider. I showed them that I could do anything with children: singing, teaching notes, music theory, and we could develop an early childhood music program.

In two weeks, I received a call from the district that I was accepted, and I could start my class tomorrow, Saturday at 10 a.m. I found out later that they put my class in an Elk Grove Park District class booklet. Immediately, six more students signed up for the week ahead. I had twelve children with parents watching. A few families who had siblings had asked in the office if they could join, if I could teach piano to their kids. I started working from 10 a.m. to 1 p.m. I was earning $7 an hour, which was minimum wage, but I didn't care. I loved what I was doing.

The next Saturday I had four more students. That meant two more hours to work. In two months, I was working Fridays from 4 p.m. to 10 p.m. and Saturdays from 8 a.m. to 4 p.m., completely booked with group music lessons and private piano lessons for $7.50 an hour. And the rest, as they say, is history …

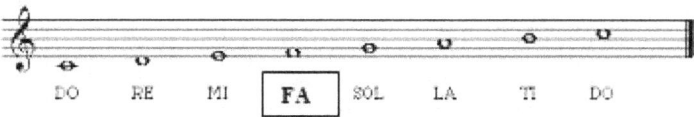

# Chapter Four
# The effectiveness of Music

**Children are naturally musical and have a creative interest**

It has been suggested by many that new-born children are predisposed to certain aspects of music (such as pitch, melody and rhythm) and that this finds expression in the spontaneous creation of simple "songs." During the first years of life these come into play with characteristic bits of familiar tunes that the child comes to learn from repetition. The melodies of the dominant culture eventually gain the upper hand, so that children (by the age of five or six) have a schema of what constitutes a song (characterised by cultural influence) and can reproduce familiar tunes fairly accurately.

This natural musical intelligence can be enhanced or restricted by circumstance, including provision or lack of opportunity; positive or negative influences exerted by family and peers; early success or failure shaping the individual's perception of their ability; and conflicting interests.

There are three things that music teachers can do to foster musical creativity among their students.

First, they can help students develop vocabularies of musical patterns by exposing them to many different, age-appropriate songs and chants and to individual musical patterns. If patterns are sequenced in this order, students will develop large vocabularies with which to create music. I successfully teach, and perform, every year "50-Nifty United States" written by Ray Charles in a chant form with my three-six years-old class. It is amazing and surprising for everybody how well little kids sing that. This song is usually performed by adult or high school choirs. I came up with a special rhythm for chanting names of states in alphabetical order and am absolutely positive that the rhythm made it so easy for young children to remember forever all the names of the states in proper order. It's fun to watch the students point on the map to a state and name it out loud in a not slow tempo.

Second, teachers can engage their students in projects emphasizing improvisation and composition, the two main creative activities in music. Improvisation should precede composition, and teachers must be careful not to give students overly detailed restrictions on either their improvisations or their compositions. However, if students are not given some restrictions, it will be hard for them to decide what to improvise or compose. Therefore, teachers should set a general context for an improvisation or composition project. This is a process that is placed somewhere between free creative work and formal exercise.

Finally, all of this must happen in a psychologically safe and accepting environment. The development of musical creativity will be better fostered in classrooms where students' attempts at creating music are accepted and the emphasis is on learning the process of creating music. In classrooms where the emphasis is on correct answers and where students are made to feel that their attempts at creating music are not good enough, the development of musical creativity will suffer.

## The twelve benefits of a music education

1. **Early musical training helps develop brain areas involved in language and reasoning.** It is thought that brain development continues for many years after birth. Recent studies have clearly indicated that musical training physically develops the part of the left side of the brain known to be involved with processing language, and can actually wire the brain's circuits in specific ways. Linking familiar songs to new information can also help imprint information on young minds.

2. **There is also a causal link between music and spatial intelligence (the ability to perceive the world accurately and to form mental pictures of things).** This kind of intelligence, by which one can visualize various elements that should go together, is critical to the sort of thinking necessary for everything from solving advanced mathematics problems to being able to pack a book-bag with everything that will be needed for the day.

3. **Students of the arts learn to think creatively and to solve problems** by imagining various solutions and rejecting outdated rules and assumptions. Questions about the arts do not have only one right answer.

4. Recent studies show that **students who study the arts are more successful on standardized tests** such as the SAT. They also achieve higher grades in high school.

5. A **study of the arts provides** children with an internal glimpse of other cultures and teaches them to be empathetic towards the people of these cultures. This **development of compassion and empathy**, as opposed to development of greed and a "me first" attitude, provides a bridge across cultural chasms that leads to respect of other races at an early age.

6. **Students of music learn craftsmanship** as they study how details are put together painstakingly and what constitutes good, as opposed to mediocre, work. These standards, when applied to a student's own work, demand a new level of excellence and require students to stretch their inner resources.

7. In music, a mistake is a mistake; the instrument is in tune or not, the notes are well played or not, the entrance is made or not. It is only by much hard work that a successful performance is possible. **Through music study, students learn the value of sustained effort** to achieve excellence and the concrete rewards of hard work.

8. **Music study enhances teamwork skills and discipline.** In order for an orchestra to sound good, all players must work together harmoniously towards a single goal, the performance, and must commit to learning music, attending rehearsals, and practicing.

9. **Music provides children with a means of self-expression.** Now that there is relative security in the basics of existence, the challenge is to make life meaningful and to reach for a

higher stage of development. Everyone needs to be in touch at some time in his life with his core, with what he is and what he feels. Self-esteem is a by-product of this self-expression.

10. *Music study develops skills that are necessary in the workplace.* It focuses on "doing," as opposed to observing, and teaches students how to perform, literally, anywhere in the world. Employers are looking for multi-dimensional workers with the sort of flexible and supple intellects that music education helps to create as described above. In the music classroom, students can also learn to better communicate and cooperate with one another.

11. **Music performance teaches young people to conquer fear and to take risks.** A little anxiety is a good thing and is something that will occur often in life. Dealing with it early and often makes it less of a problem later. Risk-taking is essential if a child is to fully develop his or her potential. Music contributes to mental health and can help prevent risky behavior such as teenage drug abuse.

12. **An arts education exposes children to the incomparable.** [5]

## Exposure to other cultures through music

Music is a universal language. In our Montessori class we introduce multiculturalism through the puzzle maps of different countries. We continue this work when we begin singing the songs of other cultures. Exposing children to the music, songs and dances of other cultures should simply be another aspect of the music and movement program, integrated quite naturally on a daily basis. In the home setting, where only one language is spoken, it is a good idea to expose children regularly to the sounds of another language through music.

Why is it a good idea? Young children learn by being actively involved in the process, through exploring and experimenting, through copying and acting out. And so it is with learning music, including the music (and language) of another culture, the foundations for which are best learnt while developing primary language. As such, a successful early childhood music program must incorporate movement (including dance) and should quite naturally involve learning across the curriculum. In other words, through music the child can also develop language, mathematical concepts and physical development as well as social and emotional outcomes. Music, of course, is not exclusively reserved for the school domain. At home or in a childcare centre music, including music from other cultures, should form part of the structure of everyday play. EVERY child has the right to a musical education. Like other forms of verbal and non-verbal communication, exposure to music should start at birth and even before.

It is important to bear in mind that not every child will naturally take to singing or learning to play a musical instrument. Physical expression through dance and drama is the way some children prefer to enjoy their musical experience. How wonderful to extend that experience by using the dances, the music and the costumes from another culture. And what child doesn't love dressing up?

In musical interpretation there should be no pressure on the child to "get it right" because there is no right or wrong but simply the joy of participation. When a child feels successful at something the child gains enormous confidence. This is critical where children are suffering from low self-esteem due to poor academic achievement. The more you can extend the creative arts experience, therefore, the better.

## The Rhythm of Learning

Furthermore, by exposing children to other cultures in a positive way, they gain understanding and learn acceptance of others. They need to be made aware that somewhere in another corner of the world are children just like them. These children are also having fun by singing songs, chanting rhymes, playing games and dancing. In this way inherent social values are gained, especially discovering that difference simply means diversity. Thus, it encourages a sense of harmony and inclusion rather than discrimination and distrust.

Studies show that exposing children to the sound, rhythm and intonation of language and music from diverse cultures assists them to discriminate between sounds which assist with the acquisition of language skills. Listening is a skill that needs to be taught, as opposed to hearing which is a sense we are born with. Listening to the sounds of another language encourages concentration. In time, it starts to make sense, in the same way that as babies, we all learned to understand the spoken word. Introducing children to Languages Other Than English (LOTE) cannot start soon enough. Far from confusing children, learning another language actually enhances the learning of their mother tongue.

Unlike adults, children absorb the language of another culture easily. Children who come from bi-lingual households quickly learn to discriminate between the two languages and use them both appropriately. They soon become aware that communication, in whatever form, gets them what they want.
Whether in a classroom, a nursery or at home, children are naturally attracted to the sounds of another language. Most adults can remember the foreign songs that they learnt at school. How many English songs from school can we remember? And why limit it to songs? Include finger plays, dances and relaxation music. To the child it is not important what the words mean as the music conveys the mood and that is everything.[6]

*Margarita Shvets & Raymond Aaron*

## Work ethic and practice

Music is a very interesting thing. Its ability to draw emotion from deep within us, create excitement, and bring inspiration all appeal to our right brain— both as listeners and performers. But music is also incredibly left brain in nature. It is ordered, regimented, and disciplined. This duel nature is, I believe, what makes music such a strong force for cognitive growth. We engage our whole brain in actively listening to music—and more so in actively performing it.

There is discipline and structure in the composition of music and in its study, perfecting, and performance. Neglecting structure on the composition side generally produces an undesirable product. Neglecting discipline in its performance also creates disastrous results.

It is in our practice time that we develop the work ethic necessary to consistently produce disciplined performances.

Creating music requires a great deal of focus on many things simultaneously: pitch and rhythm, reading and interpretation, fine motor skills, listening, etc. Aristotle said, *"We are what we repeatedly do. Excellence, therefore, is not an act, but a habit."* Undisciplined rehearsals yield undisciplined performances. Practice lacking in disciplined fundamentals yields poor musicianship. We are what we do.

The lesson learned by music students is that in order to attain excellence in music (and by transference, excellence in any aspect of life) you must develop a routine of focused attention to the fundamentals of your craft. We all know people who make a habit of getting by on the least amount of work; for whom excellence is seldom, if ever, achieved. Music has a higher standard. Audiences do not accept performances with only 70% accuracy, for example. We must realize excellence every time.

Music students are often high achievers academically. They have the personal discipline and focus needed to study for long periods of time. The work ethic developed during personal practice, lessons, and rehearsals becomes a part of their character. And this strength of character brings successes in every future challenge in which they engage.[7]

[5]http://www.childrensmusicworkshop.com/twelve-benefits-of-music-education/

[6]http://teaching.monster.com/benefits/articles/4143-multicultural-music-in-early-childhood

[7]http://davidahrens.us/soundeducation/2010/10/30/12-life-lessons-learned-studying-music/

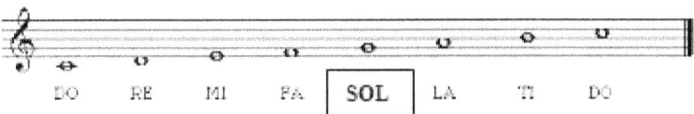

# Chapter Five
# The Montessori approach to music

## Montessori Bells

The goal of Montessori education is to develop to the fullest the three aspects of the child's nature—body, mind, and spirit. Learning music happily involves all three of these dimensions and can, therefore, be a highly integrating force in the development of the child's personality. Music-making involves a physical activity (moving, singing, playing), produced by mental direction (matching a pitch or rhythmic pattern), to convey a sentiment or idea.

Since music is a language—the movement of sounds through time to express an idea—its assimilation by the child follows the same sequence as that of the mother tongue.

- Absorption through listening, before the speech mechanism is expressive;
- Mimicry/babbling/articulation of first words, phrases, and sentences;
- Written and read language.

This sequence gives us a powerful tool, like a pedagogical outline, for preparing the 'musical environment' for the young child. The Montessori Bells, pictured above, play a significant role in this.

Because modern neurological research tells us that the ear begins to function in utero about the fifth month of pregnancy, an expectant mother can expose her developing fetus to music before birth through singing and rocking. The newborn needs a matrix of silence into which musical sounds are introduced (rhymes and ditties, repeated again and again) and stillness into which rhythmic movement is introduced (bouncing, pat-a-cake, rocking, clapping). The parents are initially the most effective persons to do these activities with the child, for they involve bonding, thereby inducing security and health.

When the child enters a Montessori preschool environment, the use of music as a spontaneous expression continues and the teacher gradually introduces the 'elements of music' in a more structured way.

*The Rhythm of Learning*

- **Rhythm:** Beginning with the walking on the line and progressing to other natural expressions of movement, such as running, skipping, and galloping, the child begins to associate certain rhythmic figures with bodily movements. Also, through the use of echoes, both verbal and rhythmic (clapping, tapping knees, snapping) children acquire a vocabulary of simple rhythms.

- **Pitch:** Through daily singing of songs, nursery rhymes and finger plays, children begin to acquire a sense of pitch. The Montessori Bell material affords the child the opportunity to hear musical sounds in isolation, to match, grade, and name them. Work with both the pentatonic and diatonic scale patterns gives exposure to different pitch relationships, which are the building blocks of melody.

- **Timbre:** Children are introduced to the instruments of the orchestra, with their various tone qualities, and learn the names of the instruments and their respective sounds.

- **Intensity:** Children hear pieces with different gradations of volume, a quiet lullaby, a strong march.

- **Form:** Children realize through listening to selected music that there is a form to music, just as there is a form (syntax) to language.

- **Culture:** As teachers introduce music, whether vocal or instrumental, its place and time of origin is given so children begin to relate music to history and geography.

When the child moves into the Montessori Elementary level, all the above elements are continued in more detail, with the addition of notation. Using the movable staff material the child learns how to make permanent the tunes he/she has invented.

This notation material performs the same function in music that the movable alphabet does in language. Increasingly, music is allied to its cultural roots and is studied as an expression of ethnicity and as part of the fabric of a given culture at a particular time. The children study the heroes and heroines of music and make timelines of composers to discover how musical forms and styles have evolved through the ages.

What is the expected result of a thorough experience of music from birth through the school years? The philosopher Susanne Langer has said, "What discursive symbolism language in its literal use does for our awareness of things about us and our own relation to them, the arts do for our subjective reality feeling and emotion, they give inward experiences form and thus make them conceivable." Emphasis on the developing cognitive skills must concurrently go with attention to the child's affective life, the inner thoughts and feelings. Through regular exposure to the great music of the past and present, the child has touchstone with his/her own inner life of the spirit.[8]

**Rhythm training**
I can scarcely think of anything more fundamental to musicianship than rhythm. With few exceptions, I find that a solid rhythmic foundation is truly the root of a good performance. A piece played with otherwise flawless accuracy sounds sloppy or even falls completely apart without proper rhythmic control; never mind if the notes were pitch perfect, the dynamics were masterful and the ornamentation was authentic. I feel this is true regardless of ensemble size, style or instrumentation. A choir/orchestra with 100+ members needs to hold together with precision, as does a small ensemble with just a handful. Even an unaccompanied soloist playing in a very free, rubato style must have a strong sense of pulse to deliver her musical message most effectively.

*The Rhythm of Learning*

Like so many things in music, the basics of solid time and rhythmic notation and accurate interpretation can be explained in a few hours and perfected over the course of one's entire life. While the elementary process of counting correctly can be summarized in just a couple of pages in a basic theory or method book. I find that students of all levels often struggle with the finer points. Even if they understand the system intellectually, it can take years to internalize. I have some exercises and ideas I have learned over time and utilized in my own playing that I have also used to help students who have consistent trouble reading rhythms and/or playing in time.

**Feeling the pulse**
A lot of people might believe they have "no sense of rhythm," but this is seldom true. Supposedly, only about 4% of the population is "beat-deaf," a form of congenital amusia similar to tone-deafness. If a student has unusual trouble keeping time, it is far more likely that they need more time practicing the basics. Demonstrate the concept of pulse to beginning students by having a student clap along with the beat when you play a very simple song in a basic meter. If they have problems you can clap with them along to a recording, or tap their arm lightly to emphasize the kinesthetic element of the pulse. Encourage your student to practice clapping or tapping along to match a metronome set at a medium tempo.

**Rhythmic ear training**
Set the metronome to an easy, medium tempo. Clap or play a simple rhythmic figure on one note for one or two measures, then repeat. Have your student rest for a measure and then clap/play exactly what they hear. This exercise can be turned into a basic call-and-response-style improvisation game. If you keep your rhythmic figures extremely simple you can also ask your students to transcribe what they have heard–this should be a rhythm-only dictation exercise at first, and can start as soon

as they have a grasp on the basics of reading quarter notes/half notes and rests in common time.

However, I prefer to use Flash Cards in this instance: What I do is I show them half notes, then the next card will have the quarter and the eighth notes, the first going ta ta ta, then ti ti ta, back and forth until they get the rhythm, the next one going tol and then ti ti rest ti ti rest. At the beginning they just click on the notes then we show the next card. They learn to read ahead and to match the sounds with the ear.

When they get to this stage I sit them in a circle and they see four cards. They look at the cards as I tell them I'm going to take one away, and then I take one away. So they are listening to me and reading at the same time. Then they close their eyes while I take the card away and then they open them and tell me which one is missing (they clap it, actually). This is the most fun part. And it lays the way for them to actually begin writing their own songs.

So, whatever they clap, they can write it down. Thus, first comes ear recognition, then comes memorization and then they produce the song. At this point I give them an instrument to play. So, instead of just banging on the Xylophone, they play the rhythm of whatever card I give them. So it might be ti ti ta. It makes no difference what note they play, it's the rhythm that gives them the sense that they are playing a song.

In the ages three to six class they then use the cards to write their own song, using the cards in any order or even making up their own cards.

In the Montesorri class everything is available 24/7. The child chooses what he wants to work on, so you show them, leading them to the step where they recognize the activity, then they go on to doing the activity themselves.

**Breaking down trouble-spots in music**

One year (2004-5) I had absolutely talented whole class. We organized the Folklore singing Group, the "orchestra," the Music Play or "Musical, "The Movie production." We recorded a real movie with my class! When we worked on Winter Concert to perform "Christmas Carols" using all instruments: metallophone, xylophones, even recorders, keyboard, bells, sticks etc. It was a lot of challenges during practice.

When I encounter a difficult rhythmic passage in a new piece of music, I ask my students to put their instruments down and attempt to tap, clap, or sing the rhythm—this way they can focus solely on dissecting the rhythm and not worry about things like tone production or technical limitations of their instrument. This technique works well with large ensembles as well; for example, I usually ask wind ensemble sections to set their instruments aside and "sizzle" the rhythmic figure by whispering an "s" sound. This has an advantage over clapping as the group can hold notes as written and approximate articulation as it would happen on their instrument. Plus, the overall effect is equally as humorous as (while being a bit less cacophonous than) the sound of a dozen fifth grade trumpet players attempting to clap in unison or sing their parts a capella.

## Counting with underlying subdivision

Breaking down a rhythmic phrase to its smallest common-denominator is an excellent way to teach students how to keep their place within the measure. Additionally, it gives them the ability to figure out more complicated rhythms and syncopations on their own. For example, a 4/4 passage containing quarter and eighth note values but no sixteenths can be clapped, tapped or spoken against the background pulse of eighth notes ("one-and-two-and-three-and-four-and," etc.). While you may want to start the process by counting out the subdivision while the student attempts to clap on the appropriate part of the beat, eventually the exercise will be most helpful when the student counts the subdivision aloud while clapping their part. Alternatively, you can ask a student to conduct while speaking the appropriate rhythm aloud (e.g. two eighth notes followed by a dotted quarter followed by two more eighth notes in ¾ time becomes "one-and, two, three-and").

## Supplemental rhythm-reading assignments

Of course, reading music requires practice for one to achieve fluency. As a musician gains experience, they will develop a vocabulary of common rhythmic phrases which become instantly recognizable, akin to common phrases and idioms in any spoken language. In addition to standard repertoire and technical exercises, supplemental rhythm-only drills can be assigned to students of all levels—this will augment their reading abilities and sense of timing and add variety to their practice routine. Some method books contain special sections with counting/rhythm-reading exercises. Beyond that, there are a few useful standalone texts and collections of exercises I have found.

## Hands-on Voice training

All Montessori material in the classroom is hands on material. The child doesn't learn by their eyes only. The child doesn't do what you tell him to do, the child copies what you are doing and he learns with his hands. Every time he touches or is moving his hands the muscle memory is connected to his brain memory. The hand signs showing where the music melody is going has been very helpful. My master's degree in music and knowing the music system of Karl Orff and Zoltan Kodai is what has allowed me to teach my class with the hand signs on every scale step of the music.

And I found a great way for children to remember this and to distinguish where the melody goes. So my first lesson on the steps in music is on the fifth and the third step. And we have a lot of fun making the Kuckoo Bird song and asking for their name by singing "What's your name?" on the fifth, fifth and third step. Then they answer, "My name is ___." and that is a great introduction to the lesson since I tell them that this is a music lesson so instead of talking we will be singing the words. So, I tell them I am going to ask your name by singing my tune and you are going to answer your name by singing your own tune using the fifth and the third step. Next I use the sixth step. And the tune of "Rain, rain go away come again another day," and on "another day" we go to the sixth step and show with the hand. The kids become fluent quickly. Gradually I introduce other steps of the scale in order of second step (degree of major scale, then forth and seven). Later we begin singing easily a capella means with no instrument support at all. Knowing the music signs help children to learn the new tunes easily.

## Intro Piano

When I put the piano in my classroom, I decided to introduce playing the piano to the whole class. First I set up the rule: one finger at a time and one key at a time. That was the simple ground rule for using the piano during work in the class. We learned the pattern of two and three black keys. The "Blind Keys" exercise helps every child to learn how to be "very gentle and respectful with piano keys and any other instrument." After a "Geography on the keys" exercise we play: The white key on the right or left of two or three black keys with the third (middle) finger only and right-left hand motion. I invited one child at a time to play on the high keys with the right-left hand motion, just two chosen keys while making an accompaniment with the first, sixth, fourth and fifth chords on the lower notes. Every child got super excited playing E-C or E-D-C in different order and listening to a simple tune "made by themself."

Every year I have two to three students who came up with nice melodies of their own and then start to seriously take piano lessons. Whenever I have had a classroom observer, the most impressive part of the observation has been when a child spontaneously went to the piano and played a simple tune with "eyes on the music ... reading notes ... then making a very nice melody of his or her own.

[9]

## Creative variation for making music

The cards are used to play a simple tune. Children play on the keyboard on e-c-c, and then they play a simple tune themselves. They put the rhythm cards on the piano and play on any keys, so it could be ... me re do me re do mi mi, which become the melody or song.

## Note flower voice training

Note flower voice training uses a huge, windmill-like flower. They like to see the flower petals revolving. They will look and memorize and repeat the single sounds. This is how they learned to read. I use my five fingers like the five lines, so that I can show them the order of the notes, like c d e, etc. So, one will grab a petal. Let us suppose it is G; so we will start repeating the notes on the five fingers, beginning with G. They also learn intervals and chords at four years-old. The first is a fighting interval—it's close together. The second is two friends arguing—not so close together. The third is forceful like a brave person, and the fifth is like a spaceman.

## Note Flower

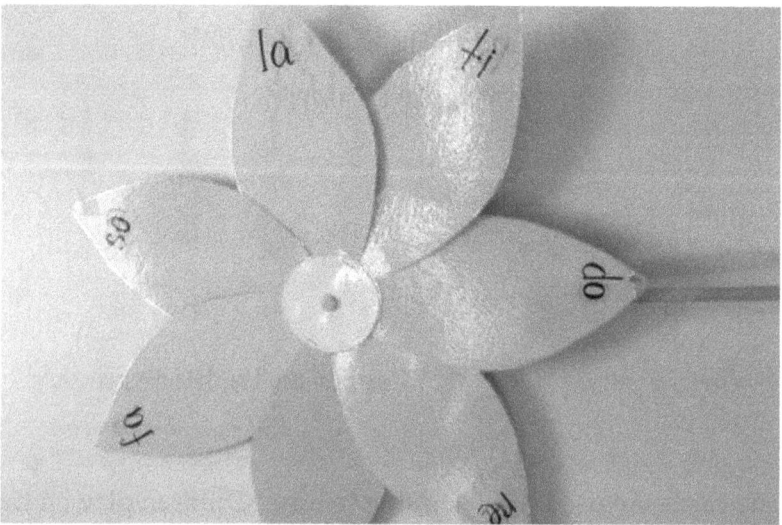

I love using the "Note Flower" in my class. The huge size makes it attractive for children, and when the petals are each a different colour it makes it even more noticeable. The petals have the note names: do, re, mi, fa, so, la, ti and, on the other side of the flower, they have A, B, C, D, F, G. Singing the notes (the scale or just two to six notes in the row) helps children to remember the order of the notes, the names, what comes next or even learning steps, skips, intervals, chords, etc. They love to spin the flower like a windmill and grab one petal with eyes closed and then start their line of notes from that position.

Any classroom can have it, because you can make one of the flowers from post board and a small wooden stick with a tiny nail (very loose, so that connected petals will spin easily) in the middle to hold the flower.

[8]http://www.tchmontessori.ca/public/?Content=Music

[9]http://mariamontessori.com/mm/?p=1692

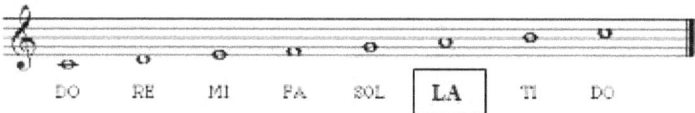

# Chapter Six
# Why every day?

- **As mentioned in a previous chapter, a drop of water, repeated many times, can wear away stone.** So too can a stone cutter cut a stone in half by continuously pounding on the same spot, time and time again, until with one final strike of the hammer the stone falls open before him. This same idea has great merit when teaching children music. After all repetition is the mother of skill. I teach them in small segments of time—five segments of seven minutes each—every day.

Brain research indicates that repetition is of vital importance in the learning process. Repetition is an especially useful tool in the area of music education. The success of repetition can be enhanced by accurate and timely feedback. From "simple repetition" to "repetition with the addition or subtraction of degrees of freedom," there are many forms of repetition that can be successfully adapted to music education. Music teachers can avoid the pitfalls of boredom and mindless repetition by constantly shifting teaching strategies and including new goals and framing techniques. Using these strategies wisely, music educators can provide meaningful, refreshed and powerful teaching and learning opportunities for both themselves and their students.

- **Short but steady instruction can work wonders in helping a young child to learn music.**

I notice that children enjoy my daily voice warm-ups before singing a song. And every day it takes us a shorter time than before—just three minutes. The clapping of the rhythm cards are still used on an everyday basis after singing the songs. We go through the flash cards one time. The first day we just clap and we say the number of the cards (presentation). The next day I will use recognition in that they must recognize the card I pick and play it on an instrument. On the third day I will tell them to pick one and read it and name it. It is similar to Montessori sandpaper letters. *I follow a three period lesson: present, recognize and then name it.*

The order of the cards are always presented the same way. I begin with quarter notes (tah) and eighth notes (ti-ti), then I mix them up. Next I go to half notes and I call them tah-ah. They will be mixed with the quarter and eighth notes. Until I know they are done with them I use seven cards at a time. Then I add the whole note (Tah-ah-ah-ah). Then I add the rest. Later on the other symbols are added: the 16th, the half, the whole rest and the triplet.

- **Repetition is mother of mastery.**

    The simple act of repetition can serve as an agent of musicalization. Instead of asking "What is music?" we might have an easier time asking "What do we hear as music?" And a remarkably large part of the answer appears to be: "I will know it when I hear it again."

    Elizabeth Hellmuth Margulis' book, *On Repeat: How Music Plays the Mind* is the first place I've encountered the idea that repetition is music's most basic defining quality. I think she's absolutely right.

    Cultures all over the world make repetitive music. The ethnomusicologist Bruno Nettl at the University of Illinois counts repetitiveness among the few musical universals known to characterize music the world over. Hit songs on American radio often feature a chorus that plays several times, and people listen to these already repetitive songs many times. The musicologist David Huron at Ohio State University estimates that, during more than 90 percent of the time spent listening to music, people are actually hearing passages that they've listened to before. The play counter in iTunes reveals just how frequently we listen to our favourite tracks. And if that's not enough, tunes that get stuck in our heads seem to loop again and again. In short, repetition is a startlingly prevalent feature of music, real and imagined.

    Not only is repetition extraordinarily prevalent, but you can make non-musical sounds musical just by repeating them.

The psychologist Diana Deutsch, at the University of California, San Diego, discovered a particularly powerful example—the speech-to-song illusion. The illusion begins with an ordinary spoken utterance, the sentence: "The sounds as they appear to you are not only different from those that are really present, but they sometimes behave so strangely as to seem quite impossible." Next, one part of this utterance, just a few words, is looped several times. Finally, the original recording is represented in its entirety, as a spoken utterance. When the listener reaches the phrase that was looped it seems as if the speaker has broken into song, Disney-style.[10]

- **Range of expansion of voice.**

    The vocal exercises are: Do the very low sound on the piano and then copy what she does. It's like a groan. The kids love making the sound. We also use the hand to show where the sound is being made, by touching the vocal chords. Then we go very high, almost like a squeak. So, it is fun but it also expands their range, it makes it very easy to sing in the middle. We use it as an exercise each day to get to what we call their singing voice.

    Ee ee Yah teaches three steps on the scale.
    Ya hah hah hah comes next, making the diaphragm work.
    Mommy made me eat my M&M is also an exercise for articulation.

    As time goes on they begin to connect their ear to the voice.

    Then, to make them breathe in the back they must push themselves into their laps and hold onto their legs. There's no room for the air to go anyplace else so it goes into the back of the lungs.

We also have them breathe into their stomachs (you will know how to do it when the stomach swells up when you take air into it).

Both exercises makes them use their diaphragm, but they are fun.

The exercises work so well that the children start singing. When compared to other schools that have music only once or twice per week and that don't do these daily exercises, we found that we were far advanced.

- We practice music five times each week, doing intervals of seven minutes each, done five times for a 35 minute lesson. One interval they might be sitting, the next standing (because with the 15-24 month-old children their attention span is very small. But this way they learn five new things or five new songs per week.)

**Intervals**
-The first seven minutes is vocal warm-up exercises with the hand signs. They have to be the same every day. The children are always humming or using one vowel to produce a tone and it helps the children with breathing. (I use u, ee, ya).
-The second segment will be singing a new part of a song that they are learning.
-The third part will be all about the rhythm: clapping or stamping (movement).
-The fourth part is instruments.
-The fifth part is exercise and will be the repetition of the old song (listening skills) or what we did today.

**Days**
-Day one we do the thematic songs; just children's songs, often seasonal in nature or thematic.

-Day two we do theory, learning notes and such and rhythm. We have cards and labels and pictures that we use for memorization, matching word or picture or eventually the note.
-Day three we sing and work on a musical play.
-Day four is listening skills, history, composer, musical literature, write the composer's name, listen to his music and then singing.
-Day five is singing in foreign languages and learning about folklore and culture.
At the end of every lesson we sing songs we have learned before.

## So, why do we do music every day?

Small children have short term memories, so they must be taught every day at the child's own pace in a free environment. What happens then is that the music gets in their physiology, into their muscle memory. For example, I've seen schools that have music for one hour a week. This is not possible for young children. And they forget by next week anyway.

The materials that are put on the shelves. I make the materials myself. I started to use my hand to make the signs myself instead of using the boards. Money was an issue. I also have a small space and must be creative.

- **Before he talks ... he moves**

    A young child is like a dry sponge; when you drop it in water it expands dramatically. For example, when you get a new student, he or she is often crying. I take them to the piano and we hit a key. They always stop crying. There is a natural connection to the real piano. It is an energetic connection with the instrument; it gets its energy from you. Toddlers don't sing but they will clap or hit with sticks (in a certain way). Children don't have to worry about being perfect like they want to be when writing or drawing. While dancing, we just practice being in their body and that ignites creativity, connection and community. Each rhythm is interpreted by a child in a uniquely personal way, opening them to a new sense of freedom and possibility that is more surprising, balancing and healing (I've observed that this works exceptionally well with ADD children).

Movement is medicine, it's meditation and it's metaphor. By dancing children discover it all ... Their freestyle movement vocabulary is rooted in such unexpected, fresh and always very personal ways.

- **Singing before talking? Really?**

Edwin Coppard, the author of *Your Voice is the Messenger of Your Soul* said: "Singing is natural to everyone. The body is a perfect musical instrument. Each person has a unique and beautiful voice that needs to be heard." Can you imagine a group of 20-30 very young children ages two to six years old with their mouths wide open singing, "Da-da-da ... Nya-nya-nya ... or Yah-yah," shaking their hands or their feet ? This is not an unusual, obscure ritual. I use a squeaking or a super low rumbling, gurgling sound to get a child's voice out, and later we discover the beauty and power of their natural voice and rekindle the joy of expressing themselves through song.

- **Music before work time**

    In a Montessori classroom when kids are already engaged in activity, it's hard to break the pattern of the work time. Most schools go out to music class a couple of times per week. But because I challenge myself to have a daily lesson, I have discovered the best time to have the 35 minute class is during my line time. Now that I'm not in the classes, it could still be disruptive to have me come into the classroom. So, every morning at 8:30 we have music class. Most kids bug their parents to make sure they are on time for their music class, rather than not wanting to go to school. Hopefully, in the future I will have a manual that teaches the teachers how to do the music classes. The children are much happier after morning music lesson

    The kids are happier. It's like a cup of coffee for the parents. Soft music during class time is also a good thing; soft, soft music.

- **Reading words and notes**

    This should start when the kids are six years old. My goal is to step back. The kids can read music by this time, so they can play whatever instrument they want. They understand what they are playing, so the instrument development is a little slower.

*The Rhythm of Learning*

- **The joyful experience starts with the parents.**

    When I first talk to the parents, I explain what I do (see the following step). Then I let them know how important it is to have a smooth transition from home to the school. (Especially for those children who have never been to a preschool or who have had a negative school experience prior to this.) That's why I have a calendar for them. Just make sure that you say every morning, "Do you know that you have school today and that your teacher is waiting for you and it's going to be a great day, etc." They can say whatever they like, just as long as it's positive, because children pick up on most of what you say. So if you're talking about money or the child's performance or whether or not you like the school, it will affect how the child feels, and he or she will not have a good start to the day or may even say that they don't like the school.

    Another example is if the parent doesn't let the child practice one time the child naturally feels it is okay to slack off and not practice on another day. This puts them behind everyone else and it doesn't take long for the child to decide they don't like music.

- **Let him know how exciting the day is going to be.**

    Before I present the Montessori material for the day I always start by telling them that "Today is going to be the best day, and I have something special prepared, and then we'll have music, the dream class and after your nap we'll be having the library person come in." I continue until I've laid out their day for them.

- **Child gets to feel there is so much to do and can feel at home**

    Montessori schools are all about creating a home environment. The school should look like a home, and the classes should look like home. There should be a lot of nature and natural things with a lot of practical life activities that work on concentration, hand-eye co-ordination and sense of order. They use spoons and bowls and jars. They do tasks that prepare them for holding a pencil, but they feel like they are playing at home. In the end, the stability becomes very much like home. They think they are doing what they want but a good teacher will give them parameters to work within. Instead of saying no pick something up and show them how to do it, then leave them be. They end up feeling like they are doing things themselves. Their own choices, their own creativity and it's good for their self-esteem.

    I remember one father, when I said your son was enjoying sweeping and wiping tables after lunch (being in charge). He said, "What? You make my child to sweep? Are you using the child for work? Is that what I am paying for?" It was hard to explain that it is a process of taking care of the environment, and taking care of himself which will give a child a sense of belonging or being at home, and that feeling will change the child's state immediately to a happy, exciting state.

- **Getting ready to be a star!**

    What makes the children really excited is that they are going to get to be stars at the concerts, which we tape and then have played on the local TV channel. We are always getting ready for some celebration or performance for our parents.

My friends ask "Why do you prepare concerts so often?" But we have no choice but to perform at Winter Celebration, Spring Sing and Summer Concert! Mostly singing and piano recitals go separate. The children want to do well, so we give them training so that they will have proper poise and that they will play the very best they can. The concerts are also multilingual, because the young ones observe so much more and they want to impress mom and dad

- **I want to impress my mom!**

    Let's draw a picture of your mom. Let's write a sentence under it. And then we get a story. I tell the parents not to throw these things out right away. They aren't fancy looking like other schools, where the teacher does most of the work. Not in Montessori. At Montessori it's more scribble scrabble, but it's their own. It's a process not a product. It's a driving force that is within the child

- **Don't over teach at home (let the teachers do it).**

    Don't over teach at home. I used to hear "My child is so smart, he knows all of the alphabet." Or mom would say "I practice with my son EVERY DAY on reading and writing, I give him/her special worksheets or work books to do 3-4 pages a day and I love to make projects for him, etc." No wonder, when Sam comes to class it's always hard to encourage him to choose challenging work; he wants to color or do practical life (daily living exercises all day long). I explain to parents that we do not teach children reading, we prepare them, so they start reading on their own. It's the same with music concerts. I never ask parents to practice the words of the songs with their child at home, because the best surprise for any parent is the concert where his son or daughter is singing in many different languages and a lot of songs, with the parent not knowing of the child's capability.

- **No homework? (Do it at school)**

    Parents are always asking what can be worked on at home. I tell them that when he shows interest in reading I will let them know (Maria Montessori called this the sensitive period). Then they can begin reading with him, three letter words where you point to the words and track along with your finger. But don't do it like "We have to practice reading now." If you notice her playing with a book, then sit down and read a story with her. Make it fun, not like it's something she has to do. With singing and the notes and the words, we never have the parents involved.

    When a child comes in and doesn't want to play the piano or they don't like to read, it's because parents are forcing them to practice at home. They get to school and they're fed up and they know they can say no, so they do. I usually try to talk to the parents, but some are very headstrong and think that they know better than the professional.

- **Surprise your parents!**

    I prefer to surprise the parents when we do the concerts. I have several pianos in the school, so if you see someone wandering around at the end of the day you can just say, "Go practice." We can also offer piano lessons for the children without the parents having to buy a piano themselves. So many parents will say I didn't know my child could sing or I didn't know my child could play the piano. We use the Snowman song and the Cuckoo song, because the children have to sing so high.

[10]http://www.ethanhein.com/wp/2014/repetition-defines-music/

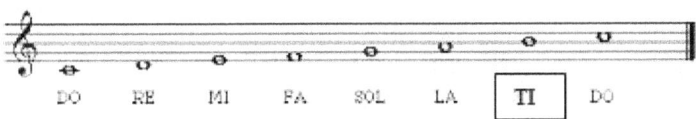

# Chapter Seven
# The Joy of Learning

- **Halloween & Thanksgiving is here**

  Halloween is a great time. We have a recital and a party. Because there is so much we can show. Even the three year-olds can sing The Skeleton song, identifying each bone. We learn all the parts of the body and we dress up. It's amazing.

The same with Thanksgiving: we sing what we are thankful for and a few other songs that we make up, and then we have the feast. We sing American folk songs like "Oh, Susanna," do tons of finger plays, naming the turkey, pumpkin pie, potatoes—all those things that we eat. We also sing about pilgrims and other different cultural songs, even Native American tunes.

- **Winter Holiday**

This is the biggest concert. There is so much we can do, even international songs. There's even dancing. It's so much fun that I can push them harder because the kids are so motivated. And of course the highlight is when Santa comes to the classroom. Even the young children can go ta ta ti ti ta on the drums, and I can play the piano, and the older children can sing The Little Drummer Boy. We also have the Montessori bells in GFGE so that we can do carols on them and also on the xylophone. They have so much fun they practice on their own.

- **Winter Concert Songs**

Everybody loved the movie *The Snow Man*. The song from this movie is written in a very high pitch. Daniel K. still could not get his voice out and connect it with his ear. His parents were saying that there were no musically talented people in their family. But in our class, after daily voice exercises with gissando to the highest point and singing 1-3-5-3-1 skipping with ya-ah-ah-ah-ah but not in chromatic order as with regular vocal exercises but with a quick changing of a lower note to a much higher note (to stretch the vocal cords) from I, then IV, II and VI etc. He suddenly got this super squeaky sound out. He ended up being the perfect SOLO singer for this song! In fact everyone gets a chance to hold the microphone and sing a part of a song. I haven't seen this done anywhere else. It's very special. And the parents don't care how good the concert is. Each parent just wants to hear his own child.

We also did *The Little Drummer Boy* to demonstrate precision. Then there was the Bunny Dance, *Twinkle Twinkle Little Star*, Build a Little Snowman and the Snowman Dance and Snowflake Dance. We had a light the candles ceremony followed by the international portion of the show: the dreidels, O Hannukah, Bel Mir Bistu Shein Dance, Shalom Chaverim, Rudolph the Red Nosed Reindeer and Santa Claus is Coming to Town. There were games and a Santa Performance followed by *We Wish You A Merry Christmas*. What a fun time.

- **Spring Sing!**

The spring sing is the most educational of the concerts. We do a jazzy version of *The Alphabet Song* and all the three year-olds chant the states—all of them. It sounds very impressive. We also do songs about nouns and other things, instead of traditional songs.

- **Solo for everyone (my voice is heard)**

This concert is actually for the three to six year-olds. The microphone is taken to each child and it's not prepared. They just sing what comes to mind or their favourite piece. The parents don't care how good the concert is, because the parents don't know what they're child knows, and they are always surprised and oh so happy.

- **Musicals too.**

   The musicals that the 4th graders in public school sing are used for the 3-6 year-olds because this is the age when they love to act. They have no fear and will have no fear later on in real life, let's say in an interview kind of situation or even on the stage. But if you don't start them now, they won't have it. My favourite is the barnyard musical. The music is difficult but fun. In the spring concert we use bugs or insects for the songs. The musicals are special, and the parents don't have to pay extra for this—it's part of the program. We usually do this in March. And the learning style we use is joyful learning.

## Music at home

- **Every child loves a drum**

   The drum is the most attractive instrument for the toddlers. They can bang all they want and get that energy out. I suggest an Indian or hand drum rather than a hammer drum (drum with sticks). To make it more beautiful; it's a warmer sound and we use cards with them, so that they follow a rhythm and so it becomes music instead of just banging. The parents are to do the same thing at home. The drum can also be used with the recorder.

- **Lullabies**

When we put children to sleep for nap-time, we use music: soft melodical or a lull-a-bye. It always calms the child down. It's good to have no games or TV at least one hour before bedtime. Do some reading for at least 10 minutes. Education should never stop.

- **Home Concerts (full attention)**

I would like to prevent children or parents from having the experience I had when I was a young child. My parents always wanted me to play something for them on the piano when they had company. I hated it so much (because they really didn't pay attention and it made me feel uncomfortable) that I got so I wouldn't play at all, anywhere. Most children love to perform if the parents will pay attention, that is being fully present to the child so that if the chance presents itself, the child can put on an impromptu concert. They really help. And it makes the child feel very important.

- **Cd players & recording yourself**

We record at the concerts rather than having all the cameras and phones going off and people standing in the aisles. These professional DVDs are given to the families. Also if the child is shown how to record at home, you never know what you'll get. The recordings are all real, not fake or put through some kind of software to make them sound better than they are.

- Everyone needs to play at least a keyboard.

I've discovered that children learn much better and with more excitement when they're younger. It's more difficult for the teacher, but there's no reason for any child not to be able to play at least a keyboard, which really helps muscle learning and visualization. We start the child at an early age and it is done in a playful manner, because they don't realize how hard it is. And because of this they stick with it as they age.

## And Going Forward?

**Build an Achievement wall**
The achievement wall is often done up as a dream board. You can prepare your child for the future by putting on the board some of the things they would like to do.
This is how it works: your child's brain will work tirelessly to achieve the ideas they give their subconscious mind. Those ideas can just as easily come from a board that exhibits their dreams and aspirations as they can from their teacher or their parents. By looking at their goals every day on paper the child virtually assures that he or she will achieve them.
Creating a dream board is probably one of the most valuable visualization tools we can offer your child. This powerful tool serves as their image of the future. It is a very real picture of where they are going or, at least, where they want to go. And

because the mind responds strongly to pictures and images, the dream board will actually strengthen the child's emotions with respect to the subject matter on the board. As they say, a picture is worth a thousand words.

**How to create a dream board**
Help the child find pictures of what they want to attract into their lives. Use photographs, magazine cut-outs, pictures from the Internet—whatever excites them. Be creative. Include anything that speaks to the child. You can, and probably should, include a photo of the child at a happy time in their lives.

Dream boards can be used to depict goals and dreams in all areas of life or in just one specific area. Keep it neat, so that the child really enjoys studying the board.

**How to use the dream board ...**
Leave it standing in an open position and have the child spend some time with it at the beginning and the end of the school day.

Keep goals that are reached on the board and add new ones as they arise. Remember to celebrate the achievement of each child as they reach particular goals. It's a good idea to create a new dream board each year. As the child continues to grow, evolve and expand, their dreams will too. Remember to have a section of the board for each area of life: family, friends, health, school and so on.

## The Power of Music

### 1. Boosts brain power
Do you want to give your child a mental advantage? Music can do that. There are many studies that show higher academic achievement happens when children are exposed to music. It stimulates parts of the brain that are related to reading, math, and emotional development.

### 2. Improves memory
Further research has shown that participation in music at an early age can help improve a child's learning ability and memory by stimulating different patterns of brain development. There is also, of course, the issue of muscle memory, which we have discussed previously.

### 3. Helps them socially
Picking up an instrument can also help your child break out of their social shell. Socially, children who become involved in a musical group learn important life skills, such as how to relate to others, how to work as a team and how to appreciate the rewards that come from working together. It also aids in the development of leadership skills and discipline.

### 4. Builds confidence
If you want your child to develop their confidence, learning to play a musical instrument can help. They will find that they can develop a skill by themselves that they can get better and better at.

### 5. It teaches patience
We live in a world of instant gratification, but *real* life demands having patience. When you are playing in a band or orchestra (and most musicians do), you have to be willing to wait your turn to play, otherwise the sound is a mess. That inadvertently teaches patience. You need to work together in a group to make music.

### 6. It can help them connect
Who doesn't sometimes feel a little disconnected from their lives? Music can be a much-needed connection for kids (and adults too!). It can satisfy the need to unwind from the worries of life, but unlike the other things people often use for this purpose, such as excessive eating, drinking, or TV or aimless web browsing, it makes people more alive and connected with one another.

### 7. It's constant learning
In some pursuits you can never truly learn everything there is to know. Music is like that. It is inexhaustible; there is always more to learn.

### 8. It's a great form of expression
People pay a lot of lip-service to expressing yourself. But how can kids really do that? One great way is through the arts—like music. It gives pleasure and expresses nuances of emotional life for which there are no words.

### 9. It teaches discipline

To improve in music you have to not only do well in classes, but devote time to practicing outside of the lessons too. That requires discipline. Exposing kids to musical instruments is the key. They are naturally curious and excited about them, and the discipline that parents AND kids learn by sticking with it is a lesson in itself.

### 10. It fosters creativity

Above all, playing music, particularly as kids get to more advanced levels in it, is a creative pursuit. Creativity is good for the mind, body and soul.[11]

## What can art do for a young mind?

That expression is a little misplaced. It should read "What can't art do for a young mind?" Art is a gateway to intellectual development that far transcends many of the other ways our young minds will get stretched and exercised in school. We live in a time where there is a war on art. Art programs, whether once a part of the regular curriculum, before school or after school, or extracurricular are falling by the wayside because schools cannot afford them. This is a tragedy beyond tragedy. The most common misconception about art is that it is inspired by culture. The simple truth is, art is created as a reaction to culture, and in turn portrays an image that is more desirable. Then, following the trail of passion through art, our culture redefines itself to suit the palettes of our leading artists. Today, too many youths live in communities that do not encourage personal development through art. It is crucial to impart a sensibility of effort and ingenuity in every single young person. They are our future and our greatest resource. Helping them cultivate their talents through art will build street smarts, academic smarts and business smarts as they take on the world they have inherited. But art in all forms is far more than just an inspiration to use your talent. It's more than education and empowerment; it's about keeping mentally fit so you can succeed to your full potential. One of the ways that we can best support our youngest and brightest is to have them sing—even if they are still unable to grasp or comprehend the language around them. Why? Singing is an expression of the soul. Long before we can directly communicate with our children, we can encourage them to develop good habits that will follow them all the way into adulthood. Singing, and promoting proper vocalization, will build confidence and instill in their minds that their voice is important. The more vocal our children are, the better they will communicate as they grow, which will inherently lead to better problem solving skills and a better sense of self-understanding. Singing is also a healthy emotional release—a far better outlet than one that could lead to aggression. Songs, in a child's mind, will also build their imagination. The spontaneity involved with creating melody will help children use their innate intuition to find meter and balance in their lives. The rhythm of life is all around us: a heartbeat is a rhythm, the sound of birds singing have a rhythm as does the woodpecker, running water has a rhythm, and we teachers are preparing the young souls to follow the rhythm of life. This is how it goes: the rhythm of music is the rhythm of learning which in turn leads to the rhythm of life.




[11]http://www.musikgarten.org/music_movement.cf

**And to conclude,** here are some non-music Montessori teachings for Parents …

We know that the child is taught mostly by the environment. So, when we criticize the child he learns to condemn. When we praise him he learns how to compare. When we show him hostility he leans how to fight. But when you are honest with the child he learns justice. When we ridicule the child he learns to be timid. When the child lives with a feeling of security, he learns how to trust. When you often dishonor the child he learns to feel guilty. When you show the child approval he learns to treat himself well (self-love). When you are caring with the child he learns to be patient. When you encourage the child he gains confidence. If the child lives in an atmosphere of friendship and being needed, then he learns to love. If you talk bad about the child in his presence, he learns to be bad. You do not say "don't" because the child will ignore the "don't" and do what he heard last. For example, if you say "don't run," the child will run. If you say, "don't push that button," of course he will push the button. In other words, when you want the child to become good you need to concentrate on the good things. Why? Because there will be no room left for the bad! If you say and show how to walk slowly in the classroom, then they will remember to walk slowly. And, as mentioned, when you teach a child the rhythm of learning, you will teach him the rhythm of life.

Margarita Shvets
February 14, 2016

www.ingramcontent.com/pod-product-compliance
Lightning Source LLC
Chambersburg PA
CBHW071625170426
43195CB00038B/2132